I love this new and timely book by Judi Braddy; it speaks to me personally. In our attempts to do everything perfectly, we often neglect Sabbath at our own peril. I'm convinced more and more that we must cultivate the *concept* of Sabbath in order to be more effective followers and lovers of Christ. I'm grateful to Judi for writing this book; I think it's her best yet!

Nancie Carmichael
Author, *Surviving One Bad Year*

Most serious Christians face the Sabbath-keeping principle at some point and either embrace it or ignore it. Like Judi Braddy, for a long time I struggled with doing no work and resting for one day each week. About twenty years ago I finally embraced Jesus' words that tell us the Sabbath was made *for us.* That means we need it.

Cecil Murphy
Author, *Making Sense When Life Doesn't*

Judi's book is altogether funny, wise, warm, and earthy. It chides gently, instructs humbly, and invites robustly. It's like a sage and trusted friend who loves you too much not to meddle a little and who actually knows what's best.

Mark Buchanan
Author, *The Rest of God*

EVERYDAY
SABBATH

EVERYDAY SABBATH

THE ART OF REAL-LIFE REST

JUDI BRADDY

BEACON HILL PRESS
OF KANSAS CITY

Cover Design: Zeal Design
Inside Design: Sharon Page

Library of Congress Cataloging-in-Publication Data

Braddy, Judi, 1948-
     Everyday sabbath : the art of real-life rest / Judi Braddy.
        pages cm
     Includes bibliographical references.
     ISBN 978-0-8341-2881-1 (pbk.)
     1. Rest—Religious aspects—Christianity 2. Sabbath. I. Title.
     BV4597.55.B73 2013
     263'.1—dc23
                                                              2013007610

10 9 8 7 6 5 4 3 2 1

CONTENTS

ACKNOWLEDGMENTS

For the privilege of writing this book I owe a debt of gratitude to—

- My husband, Jim, who showed uncommon patience in the longer-than-usual process.

- My understanding editors, who continued to believe in my creative gift and productive ability even during the times when I wondered about it myself—extending my deadlines more times than I deserve.

- My God—Father, Son, and Holy Spirit—whose compassions never fail, whose grace and mercies are new every morning, and in whom we find rest, both now and forever.

INTRODUCTION
THE REST OF OUR LIVES

Return to your rest, my soul,
for the LORD has been good to you.

—Psalm 116:7

Plodding my way around our local community park a few months ago, I was glad I had grabbed my sunglasses. Besides blocking the glare, they hid the tears of frustration that trailed down my cheeks. *Help us, Lord,* I prayed silently, *We can't keep doing this. It's just too much!*

What had me so overwhelmed? I can tell you in one word: *life.*

Life, of course, is made up of many things. The one that had pushed me over the precipice and out the door and into the park that day was yet another somewhat heated discussion—okay, a big blowout—between my minister-husband, Jim, and me regarding the overlap of upcoming events and how we would ever manage to merge them all. (Yes, Virginia, even ministers have the occasional meltdown.)

You see, for too many years event-juggling has been our primary pastime—ministry, marriage, friends, family, extra-curricular activities, the inevitable unexpected. How do we fit it all in and still find time to sleep? Simple. Sometimes we don't—sleep, that is.

Sadly, we are not the exception. Judging from almost every current conversation, spoken or overheard, life in most modern societies has everyone on a hamster wheel. What made matters worse for us was the fact that we had just recently taken two entire months off. Now here we were, barely six months later, overbooked and overwhelmed once again—which had me wondering, *Why didn't those recent restful benefits linger a little longer?*

As I neared the park's baseball diamond, truth hit a home run. I was officially, incurably weary—a weariness that no concentrated amount of time off was going to remedy. And I knew Jim was too. It's just that he, like most men, is not going to dissolve into a tide pool of tears over one-too-many overlapping events. Instead, he gets defensive and sullen, then eventually ends up having five-way heart bypass surgery, which is exactly what happened only a few years ago. Though the doctor attributed this mostly to his unfortunate family health history, I suspected that the stress of his high-profile position as a district denominational executive hadn't helped any. Obviously, I wasn't the only one in whom things had been building up.

It was then that we both agreed it might be time to seriously consider a full-fledged sabbatical. For those not familiar with the term, Mr. Webster defines it as "a leave, often with pay granted (as to a college professor), usually every seventh year for rest, travel, or research."

Every seventh year? Let's see—we've now been married and in ministry for forty-five years. I would say we were an ounce overdue.

Even so, it took us another five years to fit it in. Why? Jim had to strategically plan it so we would be gone only two months rather than the three originally offered, choosing November and December, since that was his least demanding season. Notice any Type-A tendencies here?

But, hey—two months are better than none. And so at the end of October we boarded a jumbo jet with the well-scheduled scheme of spending the first week reconnecting with our Midwestern roots. This included a short side trip to our college alma mater, where Jim was serendipitously scheduled to receive an "Alumni of the Year" award. The following four weeks would be spent in Europe—where no one could easily track us—then back home in early December to snuggle in for a cozy family Christmas.

Sounds like a good plan, right? It was, and for the most part, all we had anticipated—exciting, adventurous, stimulating, romantic, and, yes, even semi-relaxing.

Then it was over.

That was the part we hadn't anticipated—nor that as early as mid-January Jim would already be re-immersed in the problem-solving mode of his position while I flew around in the final frenzy of planning a major annual women's retreat. To make things more irritating, people kept asking, "So do you feel rested?"

It hadn't taken even a month to realize that if we had to wait forty-plus years for another sabbatical, we would be dead!

What am I saying—don't bother to take time off?

No, time off is essential. If nothing else, it allows us to step away and see things from a new perspective—to rest, reflect, and regroup, to reevaluate accomplishments and reestablish goals. It's just that if we don't make time when we get back to implement the new perspective, nothing really changes.

Might it have made a difference if we had taken six months or a year? Maybe. Yet how many of us can afford to do that—financially or otherwise? Realistically, Jim and I both knew even as the plane lifted off that day that we probably couldn't go far enough, nor could the trip last long enough, to permanently erase the effects of life's accumulated stress or prevent future fatigue. Our best hope was to put life on hold for a while, which we did. Sort of. Those are details I'll tackle later in the book.

The tough truth for all of us is that trying to cram a lifetime of rest into any temporary time off is not realistic. Without some deliberate plan of assiduous action, real life resumes too rapidly, and the beneficial effects dissipate proportionately.

Looking back, perhaps the greatest benefit of our sabbatical was that it lasted just long enough to reveal how much the busyness of life is robbing from us; to recognize again the debilitating difference between juggling and balancing; but also to acknowledge God's great grace and goodness in our lives—in spite of all our schedule-challenged shortcomings.

Consequently, we came home knowing that we had to find some way of curbing the craziness on a more intentional and consistent basis. But how? Like any life-altering discipline, I knew that finding the real rest of our lives (double-entendre intended) started with a major change in mind-set.

I'm a visualizer, so to me this meant painting a new picture on the walls of my heart—one that has not only green pastures and still waters but also a life-size portrait of the Good Shepherd, something so calming and compelling that every time I envision it, I'm enticed to slip away, if only for a moment.

Still, judging from that day in the park, I knew it was going to take some time to make the turn. Soon after, I started a biblical search just to remind myself what the whole Sabbath concept is all about. It didn't take long to discover why God eventually had to make it a carved-in-stone commandment rather than a simple suggestion. Not surprisingly, it boiled down to an age-old problem of human nature. Seems from the outset, humanity has too easily allowed everything else to take the place of God in our lives. Then we wonder why things don't go so well.

Why do we do that? When all God has ever wanted is to speak into our hearts rest, reconciliation, peace, life, wisdom, creativity, health, and wholeness? For that, doesn't He deserve at least a few minutes of our daily undivided attention?

I know somewhat how He feels. One of the other great things about our sabbatical was that for two months I enjoyed my husband's almost undivided time and attention. Amazing what a difference it made in our relationship. It didn't matter what we did or where we went. It was just wonderful being together with no outside distractions—another thing, by the way, that we promised each other that we would be more deliberate about once we got home.

Imagine, then, how much our relationship with God would benefit from the same.

My scriptural journey led me to more than one interesting observation. The result is this book, which offers some illustrations and addresses some ideas for altering our concept of rest and spiritual reflection in hopes of making it a daily mind-set rather than a regimented, hit-or-miss ritual. Accentuating the positive benefits of even a few minutes of downtime and devotion, I pray it offers a challenging yet sensible and inspiring approach to maintaining a peaceful inner respite, even on the days when life rages around us.

Before you begin, however, let me offer a couple of small disclaimers. First, this is *not* about planning a successful sabbatical or even about making sure you carve out a weekly Sabbath, though I believe both are critical biblical commandments, and I do offer some practical suggestions. If that's what you're looking for, there are any number of similar and excellent books that have already been written along these lines.

Rather, each chapter explores and emphasizes an underlying principle or two illustrating why and how God established

Sabbath rest from the get-go. Along with that are some specific areas of practical application that I pray encourage the mental adjustment that results in real-life change.

Second, I still don't have the whole Sabbath thing mastered. What I am discovering, however, in my desperate desire to slip space into life for what I know is essential to my spiritual, emotional, and physical well-being, is that rest falls into several often-overlooked categories. And it doesn't have to be that hard. It can even become—dare I say it?—enjoyable. But it does require the intentionality to adopt an attitude that keeps rest and spiritual reflection in the forefront of our minds, watching for opportunities to insert them even as we go about our daily duties.

I call it *sabbatitude*.

If you are there, too, then join me on the pages of this journey, starting with a stroll down an ancient garden path.

❖ 1 ❖

GETTING BACK TO THE GARDEN

Now the LORD God had planted a garden . . . in Eden;
and there he put the man he had formed.
—Genesis 2:8

Coming from a family of former farmers, I loved reading in Genesis 2 that one of the first things God planted was a garden. Surely it wasn't because after creating the entire world He needed one more thing to do. Rather, the Garden of Eden was planted with a purpose. It was the perfect environment for enjoying rest, reflection, and relationship—a beautiful and bountiful place that provided everything Adam and Eve needed for health and happiness. Most important, it was hallowed ground where God walked in the cool of the day, seeking spiritual communion with His creation.

If ever rest came easily, it was in the Garden of Eden. This makes me believe that the garden was an important part of God's plan. Otherwise, He might just as easily have placed man in a garage.

That's not to say that Adam didn't have anything else to do. According to Genesis 2:15, "The LORD God took the man and put him in the Garden of Eden to work it and take care of it." At that point, though, I like to imagine that Adam found his work simple and satisfying. It didn't yet involve the thorny issues that he and we less-than-delighted descendants would eventually have to hack through. Only after that infamous and unfortunate forbidden fruit incident did our tasks become toilsome.

To me, the garden represents a place where God's presence was a given, where after the heat of the day Adam could count on feeling the cool, thirst-quenching breath of God on his dry and dusty soul. Albeit brief, it was the only time in human history when absolutely nothing came between people and their Maker. "Adam and his wife were both naked," Genesis 2:25 tells us, "and they felt no shame."

Imagine romping randomly through the rainforest—without the rompers. This was true transparency—physically, emotionally and spiritually—and there was no disgrace in it. Even Adam's relationship with Eve and the animals was one of complete compatibility. What a concept!

Why then did it so soon become not enough? We can only assume that Adam and Eve took a great deal for granted. Even in that amazing environment, the first created couple quickly became complacent, curiously seeking companionship elsewhere. It was then that a soiree with a certain snake convinced them they might fare better figuring things out for themselves. Satan, who will do anything he can to separate us from God, had already slithered his way in between man and his Maker. This rebellion of far-reaching consequences resulted in their—and our—removal from that place of rest and relationship, both immediate and eternal, physical and spiritual.

Goodbye garden. Hello garage.

"How tragic," we're now prone to pontificate, "that our illustrious ancestors didn't realize until too late how good they had it!" Of course, one-hundred-percent hindsight makes it easy for us to point the finger of blame. But put that pointer back in its holster, partner. In their defense, they had no frame of reference.

We do.

Yet it seems we've learned very little from their mistake. Otherwise, why would we stay just as busy today striving for what got us all into trouble in the first place? Higher knowledge, worldly wisdom, material accumulation—the constant, curious quest for so many things that inevitably come between us and God, too often causing us to neglect, even reject, His gracious offer of time spent together.

The good news for them and for us is this: despite their sin, God still came seeking. Here's how Genesis 3:8-10 records it:

> Then the man and his wife heard the sound of the LORD God as he was walking in the garden in the cool of the day, and they hid from the LORD God among the trees of the garden. But the LORD God called to the man, "Where are you?"
>
> He answered, "I heard you in the garden, and I was afraid because I was naked; so I hid."

Imagine God's disappointment upon discovering His darlings in such a shameful, stressful state. Of course, being omnipotent, He undoubtedly already knew. Still, it's something that we who harbor high hopes for our own snake-bitten offspring find devastatingly identifiable.

Perhaps it will help us all to understand something important here. Nakedness was not Adam's and Eve's sin. Their fatal faux pas was the newly acquired forbidden knowledge that, rather than giving them the glorious insight they had anticipated, only made their vulnerability more visible. This created in them the inclination to hide their disobedience rather than embrace a restored relationship with their Creator.

Sad to say, we haven't gotten any smarter over the centuries. Whether we sin small or blow it big-time makes no difference. It's that same naked guilt that still at times has some of us lunging for the first big leaf. Even if it's nothing more than the guilt of our ongoing absence, avoiding God simply seems easier (or at least less embarrassing) than confronting our true condition and being shamefully exposed—as if avoidance were an actual possibility.

Now for some happier headlines: even before the fall, God had a plan in place for restoring spiritual relationship. "You see," states Romans 5:6, "at just the right time, when we were still powerless, Christ died for the ungodly." Eventually per divine providence God would send His own Son to crush that seductive serpent's head and bridge the eternal gap sin created. Today, because of Christ, we have the paid-in-full privilege to stand once more in unashamed nakedness before God—nothing to hinder, nothing to hide. In this way, God's amazing love continues to overcome our ostracism.

So why don't we? After all, it is with Him alone we find forgiveness and full acceptance. Because He made us, He knows us best and—miracle of miracles—still loves us most. Consequently, it's in those times together that He gives us the courage to face our fears and offers the forgiveness that effaces our failures. If only we can grasp this glorious, grace-filled concept, surely we'll experience a renewed desire to spend time in His peaceful presence.

To illustrate, allow me to share a little personal perspective. As already mentioned, I come from a long line of dirt-diggers. Thus, every spring something in my dad's DNA inevitably found him plowing up a wide portion of our elongated backyard and planting seeds in the freshly turned furrows. Though each season he vowed the garden would be smaller, it never was. Once he got in there, some soil-driven stirring took over until soon every available inch was sprouting.

Tending it, of course, required a great deal of ongoing discipline. Consequently, each spring and summer evening, after a long day's work at a local aircraft plant, he headed for what he called the "back forty." I know there were days when he felt way too weary to make the effort. But common to so many of his post-WWII generation, Dad's well-watered work ethic kicked in, and soon he was out there humming and hoeing. It wasn't hard to observe how quickly, along with the weeds, he began to work out some personal woes and weariness.

Truth be known, he had faced a lot of "hard rows to hoe" throughout his lifetime. The oldest of six children born to a poor itinerant farmer, he left school in the eighth grade to help support the family. Because of this, he always felt educationally inferior and anxious about his ability to be an adequate provider. In reality, my dad was one of the savviest guys I know when it came to taking care of business, both financial and spiritual.

There were, however, a few years in early adulthood when, despite the prayers and petitions of a godly mother, he sowed some wild oats and reaped a harvest of hurt, some in his closest relationships. Thankfully, by the time I came along he had recommitted his life to Christ and put down deep spiritual roots. Consequently, one of my fondest and most enduring memories is that of my work-weary father bathed in the light of a living room lamp reading his Bible every night before bedtime. As much as he enjoyed working the natural soil, tending his inner garden had long taken top priority. The result was a lifelong supply of spiritual wisdom and daily devotion to his church, family, and friends, making him my most inspiring earthly example.

Here's one last garden lesson we can glean. Undoubtedly going to the garden is always easier during the productive summer seasons. It's when the ground is frozen and fallow that we may forget and neglect it. Yet, as any avid gardener knows, a winter garden also harbors hidden life. Unseen, something is always stirring beneath the soil in anticipation of the next growing season. It's then, without leaves or blooms to sap their strength, that roots dig deep.

Likewise during the dark and dormant times of our lives we may approach our spiritual gardens grudgingly, if at all. *What can possibly be produced there,* we may wonder, *in such a cold and weary season?* With so many voices vying for our attention, we are not comfortable with the frozen silence. Yet there's a latent reward for lingering, waiting in the soul's winter seasons for the din to dissipate so that we can hear God's voice alone. If nothing else, we may find ourselves simply sitting in silent contemplation until we feel the stirrings of hope and promise for a better and more productive season ahead. In God's garden there is never an off season.

Again this brings me back in memory to my father and one of his favorite hymns. Titled "In the Garden," the first verse and chorus go like this:

> *I come to the garden alone,*
> > *While the dew is still on the roses;*
> *And the voice I hear,*
> *Falling on my ear,*
> > *The Son of God discloses.*
>
> *And He walks with me,*
> *And He talks with me,*
> > *And He tells me I am His own;*
> *And the joy we share as we tarry there,*
> > *None other has ever known.*
> > > —C. Austin Miles

Perhaps it was a similar thought that caused garden aficionado Minnie Aumonier to write, "When the world wearies and society ceases to satisfy, there is always the garden." Though she spoke of a physical garden, how much truer it is in a spiritual sense.

In the heat of life, God's garden is a place where He nourishes, refreshes, and restores. In colder seasons it's a place of protection and patient preparation. Either way, it's there we'll inevitably find ourselves falling into an amazing reproductive cycle where, as my friend Judy Rachels describes it, "healthy things grow, growing things change, change brings challenge, challenge leads to health, healthy things grow." And so it continues, season after season.

So here we are, centuries removed from Creation. And God still calls, *Where are you?* Think of it. Naked, scratched, and sin-smudged—maneuvering through our own snake-infested society—the Creator of the universe still desires to draw us into time spent together. Despite our shortcomings, He wants to keep the lines of communication open. So He seeks us out, offering a place of not only rest and relationship but also reconciliation and refreshing. Despite our faults and failings, He beckons, *Stop, embrace, and enjoy my glorious circle of shade and solitude.* Again, how beautifully this illustrates God's unconditional love and everlasting desire for fellowship with His creation!

Could it be possible, then, that a step back to that ancient garden is our first step toward "sabbatitude"? It is—*if* we can come to a couple of important understandings. From the very beginning, God was the one who initiated time together. Still today He offers us a place of both physical rest and spiritual relationship. How different life might look if we approach these times not out of a grudging sense of interruption and obligation but in eager anticipation, imagining how patiently He waits to meet us.

Still wondering when you'll ever find the time? Consider this: according to an old familiar adage, "Time began in a garden."

❖ 2 ❖

PART OF THE CREATIVE PROCESS

Then God blessed the seventh day and made it holy,
because on it he rested from all the work
of creating that he had done.
—Genesis 2:3

Imagine with me for a moment. It's the end of the sixth day of Creation. After completing the heavens and earth in their vast array, God has just put the finishing touches on man and his mate, then scooted them off with their multiplication orders. It's then that the Almighty leans back, places the tips of His thumbs together to form a frame around all He's just brought into being. "Hmm," He might have murmured (producing a small thunder roll perhaps?). "Just look how beautifully everything came together. I'm delighted. I think I'll call it good. No, *very* good! Now, it's been a long week, so if you'll excuse me . . ."

Okay, so I took a little creative liberty. Clearly, though, this chapter's theme scripture states that on the seventh day of Creation God rested. Still it's hard to imagine the Almighty exhausted, isn't it? More reasonably we conclude that, from the very beginning, God was sending us a message about the importance of taking time to step back, survey, and celebrate our accomplishments. He was also consigning a clue about cultivating creativity by blueprinting the necessary balance between work and rest. Hoping we would get the hint, He modeled the Sabbath first before making it a mandate.

For everyone who's ever wished for an extra day in the week—or hour in the day—this is it. Why, then, do so few of us take full advantage? Because our modern priorities have produced a precarious pivot.

You see, according to someone much smarter and less speculative than I, on Creation's seventh day the newly made man knew nothing yet of work—or life-related stress. Consider this interesting perspective taken from a devotional by the late theologian and author Watchman Nee. Based on Hebrews 4:10—"He that is entered into his rest hath himself also rested from his works, as God did from his"—Nee shares the following Sabbath scenario.

At his creation man stood in a highly significant relation to God's rest. Adam, we are told, was created on the sixth day. Clearly then, he had no part in God's first six days of work, for only at their end did he exist. Thus God's seventh day was Adam's first. Whereas God worked six days to enjoy His Sabbath rest, Adam began life with the Sabbath. God works before He rests. Man, to be in harmony with God, must first enter into God's rest; then alone can he work. This principle underlies all Christian service. Moreover, it was because God's first creation was so truly complete that Adam's life could have this satisfying starting-point.[1]

As far as Adam was concerned, rest was the rule rather than the exception. So what does that say to us on the backslidden side of creation? We've come a long way, baby—but not necessarily in the right direction. Nowadays regular rest, reflection, and reevaluation are more often afterthoughts. Rarely do we rise in the morning planning to take our own sweet time. Rather, the minute our eyes open we're already recapping today's to-dos. Seems we are incessantly catching up or gearing up, even during the times we would benefit more by kicking back.

Okay. Admittedly most mornings allow few of us—between work, school and family—the luxury of much leisure. Yet even five or ten minutes spent in Scripture reading and prayer goes a long way toward keeping us directed and protected. There are, after all, still snakes out there. Point is, we might actually accomplish more if we, too, regarded rest as the first part of the creative process rather than the last.

Of course, there's time during every day when, if we're to meet our necessary obligations, we have to get down to business. According to one recent online article, our minds actually love these focused moments, because they help us learn and experience the satisfaction of meeting our goals—not a bad thing. In the article Dan Siegel, associate clinical professor of psychiatry at UCLA School of Medicine, is quoted as saying, "The brain is continually reorganizing itself through experience. Paying close attention keeps the connections between brain cells strong and continually growing."[2]

I don't know about you, but I need all the brain cells I can sprout. The catch is that without some breaks and boundaries this can soon turn from a brain-builder to a brain-buster. In the same article, his colleague, David Rock, director of the Neuro Leadership Institute in Sydney, Australia, admits, "Getting your brain to focus is like keeping tabs on a toddler in a toy store. The brain is very easily distracted, constantly flitting from one thing to the next."

That's why, as the good doctor delineates, it's often such an effort for us to ignore interruptions and stay on track. Especially in our age of added technological distractions, we are bombarded by more information than our frazzled brains can possibly absorb. No wonder we're soon so overwhelmed that we're not just out of focus but running on fumes.

Add to that the myriad emotions we experience every day. From frustration over the morning traffic jam to a twinge of envy over someone else's accomplishments to the deeper relational issues we all live with, feelings stack up like building blocks. Often we stay too busy during the day to really think about why we feel the way we do—until they all come tumbling down. Makes you wonder: *Could this account for some of the increasing incidents of road rage and unprovoked violence in our fast-paced society?*

As a remedy, the above-referenced article suggests two things: Taking time in and taking time out. Now where have we heard that before?

The first involves those moments of introspection when we contemplate our feelings and assess our accomplishments. And guess what Dr. Rock's surprising suggestion is: activities such as prayer and meditation that encourage focus on internal thoughts.

According to Dr. Siegel, the benefits of this are even more far-reaching than we might imagine. "This practice also helps build neuronal connections and could reduce your risk of dementia. It's just another way of putting your brain to work."

Another study, from Massachusetts General Hospital in Boston, concurs, citing that people who employ religious meditation regularly have more brain activity in the areas responsible for empathy and memory. Could it be that besides keeping us from going over the emotional edge, periodic prayer and meditation might actually make us more considerate, compassionate human beings? Surely the world could benefit from a few more of those.

The second suggestion involves taking advantage of down time or time out. This is the opposite of focus time and different than time in. Whereas the first two require a differing amount of concentration, *down time* is passive and unstructured—a time when we let our minds meander, allowing the brain to rest and recharge. Not surprisingly, this is often the time when our creativity kicks in.

"Down time," clarifies Dr. Rock, "is when you're completely non-goal-oriented—staring out a window, allowing thoughts to just occur." He encourages letting your brain savor these times when they naturally crop up. For instance, when your mind wanders after lunch, indulge that daydream for five minutes before you return to the project at hand.

Of course, while a couple of five-minute vacations during the day may be unobtrusively beneficial, not too many employers appreciate their workers spending excessive time daydreaming with their heels on the desk—or brooding in the break room. That's why, getting back to God's example in Genesis, we need to be more intentional about reigning in at the end of each day when our time tends to be more unrestricted.

If we don't, the above-referenced article concludes, there could be serious consequences to both mind and body. "In today's multi-tasking, goal-oriented world," Dr. Rock adds, "our brain operates at a ridiculously fast pace, bouncing from one thought to another—an activity that can be harmful to your mind *and* body. Too few people know how to properly care for this mental muscle. A healthy brain gives you the capacity to think clearly and be creative and innovative. You'll also be more resilient to everyday stressors and feel happier overall."

Now I ask you again. Does this sound slightly familiar? From the get-go, the God who made our brains and bodies knew exactly what we would need to keep them healthy—thus the model. Whether or not God actually required time off to contemplate His creation, He knew we would.

Allow me another small speculative stretch here. Undoubtedly, even as God completed His creation, He already knew there would be some serious detours not far down the road. So might we also imagine that maybe, just maybe, God's personal reason for stepping back was that He knew this was the only time things *would* be perfect, and He simply wanted to savor it. Surely this is something anyone who has spent an entire day cleaning house or washing and waxing the car would understand. You just want to sit and enjoy the holy hush, that pristine pleasure before the first inevitable muddy footprint or bird blop appears. And you should.

Even more so are those rare days when, against all odds, everything seems to just miraculously come together. Being few and far between, they give us even more reason to stop, rest, and relish, if only for a few moments.

Truth is, every accomplishment begins in our brains. Look again at Creation. I think you'll agree that setting the entire world into motion constituted a pretty big job. How did God keep it all in order? He assigned each of the first six days a specific objective and sequence of events. In other words, He had a premeditated plan. Then He took time at the end of each creative increment to step back and examine it. Finally, after affirming it all, He took an entire day to do absolutely nothing but watch the world root itself into rhythm.

So what is it that most often keeps us from setting time aside to follow the Sovereign's Sabbath model? Most would sum it up in one word: work. Yet in and of itself, work is not always the anxiety-inducing culprit. As stated in the last chapter, God gave Adam work to do; still Adam didn't seem to suffer stress. Why? Because even though Adam lived where he worked, he managed to lay it all aside every morning and evening for a restorative tête-à-tête.

Remember: rest was the rule.

Let's face it—the majority of modern stress boils down to two things: we try to cram in too much and don't know when or how to stop. In other words, many of us have a hard time leaving work at work. Especially with today's technology—smart phones or IPads with e-mail access, memory sticks, and portable computers—it's all too easy to carry stress home in our pockets or portfolios.

In particular, those who find work fulfilling, even enjoyable, may have an even harder time transitioning. My husband is one of those people. As long as I've known him, he's seemed to thrive on the multiple demands of ministry, which inherently involve long, sometimes late hours, and solving sticky spiritual situations. Add to that an overactive sense of responsibility. Consequently, for years he never took time to try out a real hobby.

When he finally got into golf, I was thrilled. How many wives say that? So what if a bit of business gets done in between drives and puts? I suspect that's because—in case you've never noticed—there's something about a change of scenery that can suddenly bring previously illusive solutions to light.

According to nineteenth-century educator-author John Erskine, it goes right back to that garden concept we explored in the last chapter: "I have never had so many good ideas day after day," he stated, "as when I worked in the garden"—or golfed or crafted or walked. You fill in the blank. All could be considered divine diversions—doing something completely different from what we usually do—resulting in restful balance, not to mention fresh air, exercise, and a clearer outlook on life.

As for those who sometimes dislike their jobs, there's even more reason to retreat. My middle son, Derek—a formerly overworked manager for Starbucks whose real passion revolves around family and other creative endeavors—is one who sometimes struggled. Still one of the perks he managed to apply is what Starbucks calls the "third-place concept." It's their theory that most people have two places they *have* to go every day—usually work or school—but to stay balanced they need a third place they *enjoy* going. Of course, that's what Starbucks strives to be. (This should tell us something.) And for many it is. One friend recently recounted seeing a table at Starbucks fitted with twenty computer outlets—all occupied.

Others, like my wise son, try to be more intentional about taking full advantage of time off to pursue God, family, and personal interests. "Otherwise," says Derek, "you're stuck in the middle, plodding the same daily path." No surprise that he recently resigned to accept a less stressful (and better-paying) position.

Lest you think people who work at home have an easier time of it, consider a recent e-mail response from one of my online writing friends, Grace Fox, concerning the subject of Sabbath:

> As I've been reading through Leviticus this week, I'm impressed with the repeated phrase "complete rest" in the Sabbath context. There must be a reason for taking a total break on a regular basis, don't you think? As for me, I find it easy to justify writing my blog or monthly newsletter on Sunday afternoons if I'm home. I tell myself that this type of writing is relaxing for me. But maybe I need to give my brain a complete rest from producing words. You know, get some fresh air and exercise, play with my grandkids, invite friends in for coffee and board games. Maybe even read a good book about taking a Sabbath rest.

Grand idea, Grace. I know just the book.

Whatever our level of employment enjoyment, the key to unlocking daily rest and reflection depends on how intentional we are about applying those two important words, *complete rest,* to our unstructured hours. Yet, sad to say, rather than simply sitting down at the end of the day and unwinding with the people we love, we're too often tempted to turn right around and head back out the door. From sports to special occasions to church suppers, for many this translates into successive evenings spent attending one obligatory event after another.

Please understand that I'm not saying we shouldn't be involved in worthwhile events such as volunteering for church ministries or supporting our children in their artistic and athletic endeavors. As already stated, there's therapeutic value in changing gears and doing something different. It's just that too often we even overdo a good thing.

The way to curb the craziness is by building some simple boundaries, thereby setting a better example for family and others on how to do the same. According to David Spiegel, psychiatrist and director of Stanford University's Center on Stress and Health, periods of great activity interspersed with periods of very little activity give you a kind of mental-state equilibrium, or as it's commonly called—balance. Speaking for myself, I'm a much more family-, church-, and community-friendly person when I don't allow myself to become over-obligated. How? Try liberally sprinkling one mini but mighty word into your daily conversations: "No." That's the best one-second stress reliever I know.

Along those lines, consider another word of classic wisdom from the late much-esteemed priest/professor and author Henri Nouwen: "Our way of being most present," he wrote in his journal, "requires times of absence, prayer, writing, or solitude.

. . . Our community needs us, but not as a constant presence.
. . . Our community also needs our creative absence."

Truth is, cutting back can actually free us to cultivate creativity. You see, a large part of creativity is resourcefulness, which means taking time to recognize what we have to work with, then finding innovative ways of applying our abilities and repurposing our possessions. As a general rule we are all more resourceful when our minds are at rest, allowing time for subconscious thoughts to bubble to the surface. I wonder, *could that be why so many creative thoughts come in the shower or the middle of the night?*

The British often employ this wonderful phrase: "At the end of the day . . ." meaning, as we Westerners might say, "What it all boils down to." I like theirs better, because it indicates winding down daily for assessment rather than waiting until you have a sticky mess—or worse, a burned-dry container.

Perhaps that's why, during one of my recent devotional readings, the last portion of Psalm 92:1-2 seemed to jump off the page: "It is good to praise the LORD and make music to your name, O Most High, proclaiming your love in the morning and your faithfulness at night." I've since made it a heartfelt practice to start each day thanking God for His love and end it by acknowledging His faithfulness. No matter what transpires in between, it's amazing how much peace that routine spiritual reminder has brought into my daily life. Surely it's no coincidence that this psalm is subtitled "A psalm. A song. For the Sabbath day."

This brings us, then, right up to Day Seven of Creation—the Sabbath. It's the one day God purposed as different from the previous six, dubbing it both blessed and holy—concepts we'll define more clearly in the next chapter. For now, let me just say that that the Sabbath is blessed because it's a day set aside for contemplation and celebration of all we've accomplished. It becomes holy, however, only when we take time to acknowledge the God who himself rested on that day from all He accomplished on our behalf. This involves setting aside time to meditate on His love, grace, and provision, reflected in His creation; express gratitude for the health, talent, and ability He gives us; and seek His help in directing our efforts so that they come into conformity with His.

Here, then, are three more steps toward "sabbatitude" as we adopt His model of taking *time in* daily to reflect and readjust, *time out* to enjoy, dream, and create, and *time off* for complete rest that includes praising and worshiping God for His love, grace, and provision. Surely as we do, our days will settle into a more creatively blessed and holy balance, helping us to bring our own small worlds into order.

❖ 3 ❖

WILL THE REAL SABBATH PLEASE STAND UP?

Then he said to them, "The Sabbath was made for man,
not man for the Sabbath. So the Son of Man
is Lord even of the Sabbath."
—Mark 2:27-28

"Hurry, children, hurry. It's getting late. The sun is going down. It's almost the Sabbath."

Anyone familiar with the Broadway-inspired movie *Fiddler On The Roof* should recognize those lines spoken in the first scene by Mama Golde as she shooed her flock of five daughters and hard-working (if occasionally hard-headed) husband upstairs to change for dinner. What was the rush? It was nearly sundown on Friday, the signal for Sabbath to officially begin.

Friday?

Yep. Even today, the traditional Jewish Sabbath is observed from sundown on Friday until sundown on Saturday, which is, by the way, the actual seventh day of the calendar week. *Why then*, you may wonder, *do most Western religions recognize Sunday as the Sabbath?* It basically boils down to another thing *Fiddler* fans will remember: *tradition!* In fact, tradition is the main theme of the movie, something that Tevya, the Papa and lead character, struggles with as times change and the roots of his religion are challenged.

Likewise, on many levels changing times seem to have produced some similar Sabbath confusion in modern Christian circles. Consider this conundrum as expressed by another of my online writing cohorts, Kathleen Gibson:

> All my Christian life I've equated Sabbath with the day I worship—Sunday. Yet I recently heard a well-known pastor comment that in obedience to Scripture, he observes the Sabbath on Saturday but preaches on Sunday, [also] involving himself in other usual Sunday activities. Another prominent Evangelical leader also recently commented that "Evangelical America will fall on the sharp edge of the fourth commandment," referring to the day as well as the spirit of our observance.

To borrow a current colloquialism from my grandkids, "That's harsh, dude." Still it illustrates the wide range of emotion attached to Sabbath observance even today.

Friday? Saturday? Sunday? What's an earnest Sabbath-seeker to think? First let me assure you, this controversy is nothing new. The minute Moses laid down the law—maybe even before that—the religious debate over what constitutes the Sabbath began. And it's not because God didn't clearly define the concept. It's just that once something hits society it can quickly get convoluted and misconstrued.

Perhaps this explains why in the New Testament Jesus fueled the fire of controversy by tweaking a tradition or two. As was commonly the case, He was attempting to set the record straight by drawing attention away from the *when* and *how* back to the *Who* and *why*—something we in our own search for Sabbath rest should also regularly reconsider.

Before we get to that, though, let's shed a little historical light on the subject by taking an abbreviated side-trip back to the place where Sabbath law was written in stone: Mt. Sinai. Sad to say, in spite of God's attempt to purge the world of sin by sending the Great Flood—remember Noah and the Ark?—things on earth toward the end of Genesis hadn't really improved much. Particularly for God's chosen people, the Israelites, times had gotten worse. Through a series of unfortunate yet providential events (starting in Genesis 37 with the giving of Joseph's colorful, much-envied coat, leading to an unbrotherly bit of sibling rivalry, culminating in a severe famine), the whole clan eventually ended up in Egypt serving as slaves.

Under those circumstances, life had taken an almost unbearable detour. Still, though the Jews had lost their joy, they kept their tradition. Not only did the Sabbath serve as a sustaining respite, it was what preserved their culture in that foreign land, both religiously and physically.

You see, tradition can be a good thing in the sense of something spiritually significant and sacred being passed down. Though God had not yet carved the commandments, the Israelites as a whole had been observing His spoken law for centuries. In particular, "Remember the Sabbath Day by keeping it holy" was a practice they knew by heart, passed by word of mouth all the way from Adam. So obviously it wasn't because they had poor memories that God put the words in writing. It was because, like the childhood game called "Gossip," something important had gotten lost in translation.

How? Perhaps the plague-prodded Exodus from Egypt will give us a clue. This was an event you may remember being dramatically immortalized in yet another famous film, *The Ten Commandments*. Using some amazing special effects—especially that crossing-of-the-Red Sea scene—it gave us a Hollywood-enhanced image of what transpired.

On the other side of the sea, however, life took a dramatically different turn. There we find the Israelites pitching their tents in the desert, but they are not happy campers. Fact is, they were hardly out of the Cairo city limits before they started complaining.

With all due sympathy, having Pharaoh's army on your heels must have been alarming. Then trudging through the sand with little to eat and more than a few unfriendly neighbors, well, desert-dwelling was surely a far cry not only from the Garden of Eden but also—as they reminded Moses on more than one occasion—the garlic of Egypt. For slavery to look good, times had to be tough.

Presumably at that point, Moses' repeated reminders that they were God's chosen people seemed more a bane than a blessing—a concept that hasn't changed much over the centuries. As our *Fiddler* friend Tevye lamented to God, "I know we are the chosen people. But once in a while, can't you choose someone else?"

Even so, time and again, God in His grace gave in to their grumbling and provided them what they asked for. Then were they happy? Only until the next trial came along. Makes you wonder how many miracles God has to perform for people to have faith, doesn't it? No wonder they are sometimes classified in Scripture as stubborn and stiff-necked.

Nothing like us.

Consequently it wasn't long before God had the Israelites putting down stakes near Mt. Sinai for a short respite. His real purpose, though, was to call an executive meeting with Moses on the mountaintop.

No sooner had Moses made the summit when God thundered, "That's it! Obviously these people need some pointed precepts. It's time to lay down the law." Or something to that effect. So there with His own finger God engraved the Ten Commandments in granite.

Even then, it was forty days and a few additional laws later before Moses finally muscled the two stone tablets down the mountain. And what did he find? His impatient protégés were worshipping a golden idol. As I've often said, you can take the Israelites out of Egypt, but—well, you know. Angry at their antics, Moses literally threw the book at them, breaking the tablets into pieces.

Here's something I've always found interesting. Considering their recent track record, why did this "sudden" onset of sin come as a surprise to Moses? Yet God knew all too well what people left to their own devices will do. That's why He eventually compiled a complete reference book called the Bible. In the meantime, He sent poor Moses packing back up the mountain to chisel out a new copy of the Top Ten.

Surely it's obvious by now why these ten foundational fundamentals could no longer simply be suggestions. Suggestions, it seems, are something we humans don't always pay attention to. Take for instance my cholesterol. My concerned doctor has long suggested that I watch my eating habits and lose some weight. Despite repeated promises to do better, I didn't take it too seriously until my cholesterol levels recently hit an all-time high, prompting him to write a prescription with some pretty icky side-effects. Something about seeing it in both writing and real life caused me to finally comprehend the undesirable consequences—immediate and long-term. I knew it was time to take his advice to heart (literally) and start a long-postponed program of self-discipline.

How much more is God concerned about our spiritual health and eternal well-being? Enough to write those ten important "prescriptions" in stone, straightforward and stringent. The Sabbath, specifically, was not to be just any other day; rather, it was to be a day set aside with meaning and purpose attached to it. "A sign between me and you [the Israelites] for the generations to come," God calls it in Exodus 31:12, "so you may know that I am the LORD, who makes you holy." So important was it that those failing to adhere were to be punished by death.

This was serious stuff.

You see, God was set on not only delivering His people out of Egypt but also drawing them back to himself. He was reminding them not only of who He was but also of who they were in Him—a God-fearing nation, set apart to embody His eternal plan and purpose. Driving this deeply required drastic measures.

Now we come to the personal parallels. Despite living in today's so-called age of enlightenment, we are little different in character than the Israelites. First of all, we are every bit as much a generation of slaves. Only ours is a self-imposed slavery to society and our own stressful habits. Otherwise, why would busyness have become such a way of life that we hardly remember what it really means to take a day off—regardless of which day it is—or more important, *why* we take a day off?

Also, in case you haven't noticed, we, too, are living in an increasingly foreign culture, especially as it views Christianity. A few of the reasons I see are these. First, it seems those who choose to take a public stand on the side of biblical principles are often either completely misunderstood or deliberately misquoted by the media. Then there are those fanatic few who, due to a lack of knowledge or wisdom (or both), make complete fools of themselves and bring a bad name on all Christians. This still leaves the large majority who rarely take any stand at all. I don't know which of the three is worse. We can commiserate until the cows come home about secular society trying to make Christians look bad, but the truth is that we may be our own worst enemies. Sad to say, so many of society's unnatural norms have leapt into our lifestyles, it's hard sometimes even for us within the ranks to discern a difference, much less those around us.

What we seem to have forgotten is that though the Ten Commandments were written initially for the Jews as God's chosen people, according to 1 Peter 2:9 those who embrace the new covenant in Christ are chosen as well: "You are a chosen people . . . God's special possession, that you may declare the praises of him who called you out of darkness into his wonderful light."

It could be, then, that two of the less-ruminated reasons for modern-day Christians to resume a regular and religious Sabbath observation are, first, for the purpose of absorbing sound doctrine so that we can make informed and intelligent comments; and, second, to strengthen our spiritual resolve to model a loving but uncompromising example of what adhering to a higher spiritual standard means—not to mention the importance of preserving our Christian culture. The Sabbath is, after all, a historical part of our Western heritage as well.

Or *was.*

You see, I'm old enough to remember a time before the late 1950s when Sunday was a very different kind of day. Where I grew up in Midwestern America, most stores actually closed on Sunday—not necessarily because every employee observed a spiritual Sabbath, but the Bible-inspired concept of a weekly day of rest was still religiously rooted in our society.

On a personal level, observing a spiritual and restful Sabbath was a practice my God-honoring parents took very seriously. For us, the foremost priority was attending church. Fact is, our family went twice on Sundays, both morning and evening, not to mention mid-week Bible study and every other time the doors were open. Were we fanatics? No, just devoutly deliberate about taking advantage of every opportunity presented to worship God, study His word, and support our church.

After services we would then most often head home for a simple-but-satisfying dinner, which my mother had usually prepared ahead of time. Following that, we guiltlessly whiled away the afternoon reading, napping, playing games, or paying an occasional visit to friends until it was time to return for the evening service.

Only one time do I remember my dad doing something that broke his keeping-the-Sabbath-holy code of honor: he bought a car on Sunday. Turned out, that car gave him nothing but trouble, which, suffering much gratuitous guilt, he always believed was because he had "sinned against the Sabbath." Maybe he was right.

I suppose today some would consider all that a little spiritually antiquated. Sad to say, for many in today's society regular church attendance is no longer a tradition. Or worse, that's all it is—a sort of guilt-driven nod in God's direction. Fact is, recent statistics tell us many people today consider themselves regular church attenders if they manage to make it two Sundays a month. When it comes to preserving the practice, I can't help wondering what kind of message this sends their children. Believe it or not, I know parents who don't even require their children to go to church, giving them instead the leeway of "making their own decision when they are old enough." Interesting how they don't do that with school, medical care, or music lessons.

Those parents might be enlightened to know that when I was an impressionable adolescent, fearful in a world full of chaotic changes, church became my true sanctuary. I could hardly wait to get there, because it offered a safe and peaceful place filled with loving, supportive people. Growing up in the church also meant that my closest friends were those who shared the same faith and spiritual standards, providing a positive peer influence in my formative years. Some of them I've kept in contact with long into our adult lives. I can't imagine that young people today are any different, especially in our scarier-than-ever society. Despite the occasional negative news story, church is still the best part of a child's upbringing—a practice I'm forever grateful to my parents for instilling.

It's also worth noting how quickly many church-alienated adults run back to their religious roots when the world comes tumbling down around them. Take, for instance, when the World Trade Centers were attacked on September 11, 2001. People packed the pews, seeking safety, solace, and some way to make sense of what had just happened. Though for some it didn't last long, this still shows how deeply embedded a spiritual heritage can be. Sad, isn't it, that it takes something of that malevolent magnitude to bring us back to where we belong?

Of course, just going to church is no guarantee of an instantaneous or complete change in character. Sorry to say, another thing many of us have in common with the Israelites is a tendency toward being cantankerous and complaining. Seems especially those of my generation do a lot of lamenting nowadays over the turn post-modern churches have taken, which they feel, between the upbeat music and power-punch preaching, offers little in the way of rest and reverence. Not to mention the multitudinous mewling about today's casual dress code.

Personally I've worked at adopting a different attitude. Understanding that religious teaching has to remain relevant to reach each generation, I long ago determined that the music and method shouldn't matter as long as the message remains biblically rooted. Truth is, church today is a lot more about freedom of worship than it was when I was growing up—something we might come to actually appreciate if we weren't so caught up finding fault. Sure, I have personal preferences, but there are still plenty of places where we who crave custom and hanker for a hymn can still go to find our "fix." Bless you, Bill Gaither.

Then there's that whole manna mentality. Like the Israelites who never seemed satisfied with God's attempts to appease their wants, how often is our main communication with God more a matter of not just "What have you done for me?" but "What have you done for me *today*?" How quickly, especially when we concentrate only on the circumstances around us, can we forget God's faithful provision—maybe even miss a miracle or two. I sometimes wonder how much of our lack of gratitude comes from not taking regular time out to recount our blessings, yet another important part of any true Sabbath celebration.

This reminds me of the story of an Englishman visiting friends in America for the Thanksgiving holiday. "I've never quite understood the American tradition of giving thanks only once a year," he mused. "Wouldn't it be better if you were thankful for three hundred sixty-four days and kept just the one for complaining?"

Enough said.

I would be the first to admit that "back in the day" a good amount of guilt was sometimes attached to practicing what was preached. Consider this story Annetta Dellinger told about a season in her life when she was teaching, writing, and raising teenagers while also—as an only child—serving as long-distance

caregiver to her aging, ailing parents. During that time she received a call saying her dad was in the hospital and his many
rows of potatoes needed to be dug. The only time she had to
do it was on Sunday afternoon. So her deliberate plan, after
driving the seventy miles, was first to dig the potatoes, then go
visit her dad. Why? Because she knew what he would say: "You
dug potatoes on Sunday?"

"Yes, Dad," she assured him, "and God will forgive me."

Even today we sometimes need to be reminded that there's
a difference between God laying down the law and people load-
ing on the legalism. Truth is, legalism often has the opposite
spiritual effect. Not only is it stifling, but it's also a stressor,
which seems rather counterproductive when contemplating a
day of rest. To quote popular post-modern speaker David Ed-
wards, "When holiness is reduced to legalism, our hearts are no
longer free; they are focused more on maintaining rituals and
customs than on living out a genuine character change."

Those are the very things Jesus came to counterbalance. You
see, by the time He appeared on the New Testament scene, the
religious leaders of that day had also decided to improve on
God's Sabbath model by adding their own rules, regulations,
and restrictions—many more self-serving than God-glorifying.
Consequently, Sabbath laws had become so complicated and
convoluted that they were almost impossible for people to com-
ply with.

Several times we find Jesus and the disciples doing something on the Sabbath that sets the Scribes' and Pharisees' hypo-
critical, tyrannical teeth on edge. Take for instance the account
in Mark's gospel where they were reprimanded for "working"
on the Sabbath because they stopped to hungrily harvest a few
kernels of corn. Jesus' response found in Mark 2:27-28 quickly
put the scribes in their super-spiritual places: "The Sabbath was

made for man, not man for the Sabbath. So the Son of Man is Lord even of the Sabbath."

Jesus was reminding them—and us—that God's original Sabbath concept has always been for humanity's benefit, from both a rest and reverence standpoint. At the same time He was establishing himself as heaven's ultimate advocate-authority over everything, including the Sabbath. That was because, according to Acts 13:39, Jesus came to be the fulfillment of Old Testament law, which thankfully meant that He freed us from most of its rigid sacrificial requirements.

It was in fact because of Jesus that the Sabbath came to be part of Gentile (non-Jewish) culture and eventually celebrated on the first day of the week—Sunday—rather than the seventh. Though the Early New Testament Church attempted to continue meeting in the Jewish synagogue, the minute they began preaching about Christ they were banned. It was then they switched worship to Sunday, the day of Jesus' Resurrection, and started referring to it as "the Lord's Day."

It might be interesting to note that even then there continued to be disagreements among the burgeoning believers as to which day truly constituted the Sabbath—to the point where in Romans 14:5-6 Paul warns the Early Church about arguing over observing one day above another.

Considering all this, what is the good news for today's tired pilgrim? A lot of grace has been given to us when it comes to choosing the when, where, and how of Sabbath celebration. Sometimes this can be quite refreshing. One of my most memorable times in ministry was when Jim and I were invited to pastor a fledgling congregation in Anchorage, Alaska. Before acquiring our own building, we rented space from another church, which meant our Sunday services couldn't start until after theirs ended. Though it seemed strange at first to be teaching Sunday school at two o'clock in the afternoon, I quickly came to love this little tweak in tradition. Not only did it make for more leisurely Sunday mornings, but it also meant services concluded early enough that after-church fellowship became almost automatic, whether we headed to someone's home or a local restaurant.

Grace Fox tells a similar tale with a cultural connotation when, back in the 1980s, she and her husband moved to Nepal as missionaries. "In that culture," she states, "everyone worked six days a week and took Saturday off." Since Grace's husband was also working on a hydro-electric power project alongside a couple hundred Nepalese men, he did what they did. Therefore, when they and other missionaries on that project took turns holding church services in their homes, the only suitable day to do this if they expected the nationals to attend was Saturday. Consequently, Sunday mornings found Grace's hubby hiking through the rice fields back to his office once again.

Grace admits that at the time this rocked her firmly inbred religious regimen until she finally learned to embrace the principle of the matter. Now she has no problem taking a day of rest mid-week, especially when ministering on Sundays.

This brings up another Sabbath struggle common to pastors and others for whom ministry is a Spirit-called vocation. For them, Sundays can hardly be considered a day of rest—not to mention the fact that, like doctors, they are constantly on call. That's why it's especially critical that those who minister to others be intentional about taking another day off during the week in order to replenish their depleted physical, emotional, and spiritual resources.

The truth for all of us is this: today it's not as much about when, where, or how we celebrate the Sabbath as *whether* we do. Like the Israelites, we, too, wander a dry and dusty world, living out of thirsty, empty souls. We need a day every week reserved for Sabbath rest more than ever. If we aren't intentional about setting one aside, we'll never take time off.

So here are two more "sabbatitudes." First, we must see Sabbath rest as an issue of obedience. When we say, *But, God, I don't have time to take a Sabbath,* we are being not only disobedient but also rebellious. As my friend Elisabeth Sherwood recently pointed out, most of us would—or should—be frightened to break any one of the other ten commandments. Yet somehow we feel free to ignore the Sabbath statute. In Exodus 34:21 God spoke of resting even during the busiest of times: "Six days you shall labor, but on the seventh day you shall rest; even during the plowing season and harvest you must rest." Busyness cannot be our excuse.

Second, from the get-go God made two things a nonnegotiable part of every Sabbath observance. Beside *rest,* the other is *reverence.* So we must conclude that for any day off to truly constitute a Sabbath, it should include time spent turning our hearts toward God. Only when we adopt both aspects does the real Sabbath take its intended stand in our lives.

❖ 4 ❖

REST AS IF YOUR LIFE
DEPENDS ON IT

A heart at peace gives life to the body.
—Proverbs 14:30

Not long ago our beloved 1968 Olds Cutlass convertible barely cleared the garage door before it sputtered and died. Granted, I had noticed the red generator light coming on the last few times I drove it, but it had seemed to be running fine. So since I used it only occasionally for short errands, I did what any mechanically challenged female might do. I ignored it.

My husband was incredulous, firmly reminding me that in most cases the color red, when associated with automobiles, means "Stop."

"But the car was still running!" I pled my puny case. "So what's the problem?"

The problem was that somewhere in the electrical system was a short that was slowly draining the battery. For a while the car's own store of energy had kept it going. Finally, that daily drain sucked the reserves dry, causing the ignition to produce one last, sad click that couldn't bring the engine back to life.

Obviously, I should have been paying more preventive attention.

The next morning as I watched the tow truck drag our classic lemon-yellow beauty to the car doctor, reality revved my mind's motor. *How long have I, too, been running on a low battery, pushing myself beyond my own store of energy?* I had also been ignoring some pretty persistent warning signals in the form of fatigue, sleeplessness, aches, and angst. Kind of scary to think that one day I, too, might walk through the door, give one last cough, and collapse, not to mention imagining where my loving family might decide to tow me.

Funny, huh? Yet, in all seriousness, it could happen to any of us, especially if we don't take time to correct the things that are draining—or in some cases, clogging—us. Judging from the increasing number of media segments emphasizing the importance of taking time to care for ourselves, society's stressful ways are creating not just chronic fatigue and boiling-point frustration but also an actual epidemic of illness. Think about it. How many times lately have we heard the terms "childhood obesity," "type 2 diabetes," "heart attack," "stroke," and "cancer" mentioned in the media? While some herald from heredity, they are more often related to or exacerbated by some unhealthful lifestyle habits.

That's why a new class of legal drug dealers (commonly known as pharmaceutical companies) often appear on our television screens touting the amazing powers of pills for everything from constipation to COPD (chronic obstructive pulmonary disease). Before writing another word, let me be quick to say how thankful I am on behalf of those whose quality of life has been improved, even prolonged, by some of these miraculous medications; and we are indebted to the researchers who work tirelessly developing new and better disease treatments as they seek complete cures.

On the other hand, I also know intimately those who have become dependent on medications they hope will cure or curb symptoms that so far are mainly the result of an overactive, stressed-out, sometimes self-abusive lifestyle, or spent money they didn't have on drugs that didn't work. Consequently, experts confirm that many today find themselves addicted to prescription pills and facing an entirely different and debilitating health challenge.

According to my own doctor, every medication has an adverse side effect, some worse than others. Wouldn't it be better to avoid them as long as possible—maybe forever? I believe it's plausible if we will consider how many of our modern-day complaints might be traced back to a lack of rest and take steps to pursue our own personal remedy for that.

Lack of rest? Really?

That's right. There are so many ways our rest-starved lifestyles affect our physical health, either directly or indirectly. Consider three basics. First, we don't take the time or effort to consistently implement practices that contribute to keeping us healthy. Second, citing time restraints, we often ignore potentially serious symptoms and procrastinate seeking preventive measures. Third, we busily bypass any disconcerting thought of what the ultimate consequences might be until the symptoms can no longer be ignored, which is sadly sometimes too late.

Like the Olds, just because our bodies keep moving doesn't mean we aren't pushing them to the limit, even damaging them. Not only will this eventually catch up with us physically—but spiritually as well. According to Proverbs 14:30, our chapter's title scripture, the two are inextricably interrelated.

You see, when we allow over-activity to keep us from rest, we're bound to make bad choices. Repeated over time, these choices develop into unhealthful habits. Before we know it, the tail, as they say, has started wagging the dog. When these habits start holding the reins, we no longer have just a physical problem but a spiritual one as well. Why? Because anything that controls us ultimately comes between us and God.

No doubt that's why many of the rules God wrote for the Israelites were for their physical health as much as their spiritual well-being. Consider Exodus 15:26: "He [God] said, 'If you listen carefully to the LORD your God and do what is right in his eyes, if you pay attention to his commands and keep all his decrees, I will not bring on you any of the diseases I brought on the Egyptians, for I am the LORD, who heals you.'"

Does that mean as long as we obey God we'll never get sick? No, unfortunately we live in a sin-cursed world that makes us susceptible to every kind of evil condition. But living according to biblical principles does give us guidelines for making better choices while discouraging participation in unhealthful practices common to carnal culture. If only we will implement them.

Fact is, a few of those Egyptian illnesses *were* God-inflicted. The plagues in particular were a way of punishing Pharoah for not paying attention, finally forcing him to do something he didn't want to do: allow the Israelites to leave. But according to the *Papyrus Ebers*, a famous medical book written in Egypt in 1522 B.C., some of their suffering was self-inflicted. It indicates that the Egyptians were no strangers to sickness and routinely employed an unhealthful variety of home-remedies and rituals. From "magic water" (water that had been poured over a special idol) to the blood and fat from various creepy critters, it's quite likely that the cures they concocted killed as often as the disease. Even more deadly was the fact that the gods they worshiped had no power to help or heal.

The above information is not something I came up with on my own. Rather it comes from a book that was part of my required reading in college (more years ago than I would care to confess). Taking its title from the above-referenced scripture, *None of These Diseases,* by S. I. McMillen, explores and explained many of the things God either forbade or refined for the Israelites because they contributed to potentially dangerous health issues. Especially intriguing is how many of the physical and emotional consequences are still linked with present-day illnesses. In case you're looking for something fascinating and informative to read some relaxing Sabbath afternoon, I highly recommend picking up a recently updated version of the book.[1]

Of particular interest is how many of the regulations God laid down revolved around food. Even today, orthodox Jews observe these food-related laws, especially on the Sabbath and other celebratory days. That's why we see foods on our grocery shelves labeled *kosher,* meaning they meet both Jewish religious and regulatory standards. Even McDonald's in Israel, according to a recent television documentary, offers kosher cuisine such as the McFalafel. Seriously. But take heart—Mediterranean cooking features not only some of the most healthful but also some of the most delicious fare on earth—something we've frequently enjoyed in our travels, even incorporated at home.

Perhaps Western society needs to pay more attention since it's become obvious how much our lifestyle—in particular our eating and exercise habits—are adversely affecting our health. Though many Christians pride themselves for avoiding the evils of, say, alcohol and tobacco, many of us are "digging our graves with a spoon." More so, since 1 Corinthians 6:19 tells us that our bodies are "a temple of the Holy Spirit," we need to seriously consider how we're caring for His sanctuary. For the next few pages, let's explore a few everyday ambushes.

Consider, for example, two common terms originating in our culture: "fast food" and "convenience cooking." The reason it's fast and convenient is that a vast majority of people rarely take time anymore to eat slowly or prepare food properly.

My mom called the latter term "cooking from scratch," meaning we purchased the actual ingredients and put them together ourselves rather than buying a box or bag of something already mixed with who-knows-what—speaking of which, it definitely pays not only to read labels carefully but also to learn to translate them. For instance: "No sugar added" doesn't mean no sugar at all and often has little bearing on the fat or calorie content. Likewise, the term "no trans-fats" constitutes another similar deception.

Since few of us farm anymore, purchasing organic food might offer a good alternative. My only caution, after some research, is that organic labels can also sometimes be deceptive and provide an excuse for producers and markets to overprice. If considering the organic route, the most likely venues for honest labeling and good prices are usually reputable whole food or local farmer's markets. The money best spent is probably for hormone-free meat. As for veggies, using a good brand of vegetable pre-wash—as many of my overseas friends do—is possibly just as beneficial.

Either way, cooking from scratch doesn't guarantee that all the end results are good for you either. My youngest son, Dustin, is a professional chef whose taste and training leans heavily toward the use of bacon, butter, and other artery-clogging stuff. Then there's the Food Network's popular Southern-style diva, Paula Deen—alias the Butter Queen—whose recent revelation of her battle with diabetes boiled over into a major cooking controversy. While these fat-infused gourmet meals may taste amazing and be fine for special occasions, healthful everyday cooking requires a conscious effort toward making wholesome, nutritious substitutions. This was something about which we received strict instruction following Jim's heart surgery.

Admittedly this takes time and retraining, which again often accounts for why we don't do it. Yet taking time to cook is something that in itself can be restfully therapeutic. For me, little compares to spending a couple of leisurely hours chopping and simmering the ingredients for a savory soup—especially on a cold winter day. Along with the wonderful smell, a kind of contentment soon wafts over my soul. I've even come to enjoy the challenge of finding ways to make some fattening family favorites more nutritious.

One of my fondest food-related memories is that of our family sharing a leisurely Sunday dinner—something else that current statistics say has pretty much gone by the wayside. Due to skewed schedules and added activities, families seem to share few relaxing sit-down meals anymore, Sunday or otherwise.

Nor do we always take time to say grace—a prayer of thanks—prior to the meal. If we do, it's frequently reduced to nothing more than rote repetition. That's fine when teaching a toddler, but pretty apathetic for adults. Are we really so rushed that we can't turn our thoughts toward heaven at least long enough to formulate a few heartfelt phrases of gratitude to God for His provision?

Even those in the secular arena see the benefit. Acccording to an article found in a popular women's magazine, author and physician Clair Wheeler suggests that before digging into lunch or dinner we sit down, close our eyes, and take several deep breaths, then open them and allow a minute to actually appreciate the food in front of us.[2] Though that alone indicates no acknowledgment of a higher provider, it does at least model a momentary sense of serenity at the beginning of each meal. Combined with God-directed gratitude, this little gear change might even alter our gobble-and-go mentality enough to help prevent another disease quickly gaining popularity: gastro-esophageal reflux disease (GERD).

Another healthy habit too often gobbled up in the daily grind is some form of sensible, consistent exercise. Obviously this wasn't a problem for the Israelites. Wandering around the wilderness pretty much gave them their daily dose, plus some. Even today I've observed that most Eastern and European cultures incorporate a lot more walking, biking, and regular recreation into their daily lives than do we car-crazy, destination-driven Westerners.

As my husband recently remarked, most of us have migrated or matriculated a long way from our hard-working rural roots. Now, instead of working the fields or doing manual labor, many have sit-all-day, computer-centered occupations. Our children, too, spend more time in front of the television set or computer than they do playing outside. All are reasons it's critical that we incorporate more antidotal exercise.

According to a previously referenced article, aerobic activities flood the brain with its most important fuel: oxygen.[3] "The result," says our afore-quoted friend David Rock, "is a flush of mental energy." It also releases chemicals that help the brain produce new cells, which may improve memory and learning, in addition to reducing the risk of stroke.

"Wait a minute," I can already hear someone saying. "Isn't exercise the opposite of rest?" Yes, but it still provides restful benefits in the form of releasing endorphins—those little brain chemicals that function to transmit electrical signals within the nervous system. Research tells us they actually target our brain's opiate receptors, causing them to act similarly to drugs such as morphine and codeine. With high endorphin levels, we feel less pain and fewer negative effects of stress.

Even if you're not an avid gym-goer, here's some good news. According to a University of Illinois study, simply walking forty minutes three times a week can combat age-related mental and physical dysfunction. If we walk outside (which I personally prefer over my husband's trusty treadmill), we'll absorb more of the "sunshine vitamin," vitamin D. Why is that so important? According to Walter Willett, chairman of the nutrition department at the Harvard School of Public Health, there's substantial evidence that vitamin D can have benefits for colon cancer, diabetes, and infections. Yet as my own doctor recently informed me, there's actually a rising concern over vitamin D deficiency that now makes testing a routine part of most physical checkups.

While we're at it, there's one more way we can triple our workout rewards: make it a prayer walk. Sadly, taking time to pray is another thing that has become dangerously deficient in our deadline-driven lives.

Something else we don't always get in large-enough doses is sleep. Perhaps this is also linked to a lack of hard work or exercise, meaning we no longer experience enough physical activity to get really weary. Most likely, though, we simply have too much on our minds. Either way, anyone who's ever felt sluggish and cranky after a spotty night's sleep knows how desperately the brain needs it to function optimally. But did you know that sleep deprivation also spikes levels of cortisol, which lowers immunity, fogs memory, and stunts creativity? Some recent research even links it to weight gain.

So what's a semi-insomniac to do? Sleep experts suggest we give ourselves a firm bedtime so we're not tempted to cram in "just one more" chore. Let's be honest—most of us haven't had a set-and-sensible time to retire since we were about seven years old.

Perhaps some of us procrastinate fearing the frequent tendency to toss and turn. In that case, the same experts advise making a list of what needs to get done the next day, putting two or three "must-dos" at the top and the remaining "nice-to-dos" underneath. My added advice is to then commit that list to the Lord. Since Psalms 121:3 assures us that "He who watches over you will not slumber," we should be able to snooze soundly, knowing that both we and our commitments are kept safely in His care.

Rest alone is healing. We need to give our bodies time to rejuvenate so we don't get sick. And what if, despite our best efforts, sickness should strike? Instead of stoically steaming ahead, give it up and go to bed. Trust me—there's no point in trying to outrun the germs.

What's really sick is that we've come to the point where giving ourselves permission to rest requires a deliberate effort. No surprise, then, that we may sometimes forget to breathe—not entirely, of course, or we would all be falling into a dead faint. Yet according to medical experts, whether during times of extra exertion or extreme anxiety, we often unconsciously hold our breaths. It's another habit we need to break. Why? Other than the obvious, taking slow, measured breaths keeps us calm when we're at rest and helps us perform better during activity by providing our bodies' cells the needed oxygen to metabolize or burn fuel to produce energy. Conversely, exhalation releases harmful carbon dioxide.

Even more beneficial is breathing deeply—from the tummy, not just the chest—which opens the lungs and releases (here they come again) endorphins. Not only can these help ease headaches, backaches, and muscle tension, but according to Carrie Demers, medical director at the Total Health Center in Honesdale, Pennsylvania, just pausing to engage in ten full, slow breaths causes you to be calmer, more capable, and more energetic. My own doctor reaffirmed this recently when he recommended deep breathing as a remedy for my complaints about jet lag and travel-related anxiety. Likewise, when feeling depressed, thoroughly inhaling stimulates the nervous system, which can give our bodies a needed boost.

Last but not least on this long list of healthful hints are the two most obvious yet often overlooked: making an annual appointment for a thorough physical checkup, then not neglecting any follow-up treatment our doctors determine necessary.

Obviously, what I've attempted thus far is to provide information regarding some unhealthful habits that short-circuit our systems and offer some simple rest-related solutions. Even so, I'm guessing these are things many of us have heard before and merely choose to ignore.

So for the next few pages, let's take a different tact by exposing a few of the underlying spiritual issues that hinder us from taking necessary steps toward both physical health and emotional well-being. I can tell you from personal experience that our only hope of permanently making any necessary life-enriching changes is if we can stop seeing them only as physical concerns but recognize them as spiritual ones as well.

The first one may surprise you: we are an incredibly blessed society. *Blessed?* Someone is surely questioning. *Isn't that a good thing?* Yes, except that it means we have way too many choices. Consequently, we've also become an overindulgent society. Like a cop in a donut shop, some of us have lost the ability to set reasonable limits on ourselves.

Instead we do what any mature adult does: expect someone else to set them for us. I am always both amazed and perplexed by the news stories of those who blame the government, schools, even fast food restaurants for not monitoring things that we should take personal responsibility for.

Truth is, it can be a restful relief not to have so many options, which explains why the healthful eating plans that work best for some are those listing exactly what we can and cannot consume. Still we chafe. We want to feel good, but we don't want anyone else dictating how best to do it. Often that includes God.

When we finally do determine to take personal action, we sometimes end up undermining our own efforts. How? We are also an instant-gratification society. In our habitual hurry, we approach these longed-for lifestyle changes with an all-or-nothing mentality. Wanting instant results with little effort, we make radical resolutions that result in short-lived success.

Let me remind you of something else you probably already know. Nothing of value in life is easy or instant. Like the pearl an oyster painstakingly produces from a grain of grit, good things usually result from a prolonged—possibly even irritating—process. That's why doing a little on a consistent basis offers a better outcome than a lot in short spurts.

Again, we're talking about time, which translates into two other inner-connected spiritual concepts we're not always crazy about: discipline and patience. Discipline means making ourselves do something we don't always like. Patience often means having to wait for results. Both cramp our rest-resistant lifestyle and cram-it-all-in culture— something which, perhaps surprisingly, Scripture acknowledges. According to Hebrews 12:11, "No discipline seems pleasant at the time, but painful."

"That's right," we all agree, "and who needs pain?" Keep reading.

"Later on, however, it produces a harvest of righteousness and peace for those who have been trained by it."

Peace, huh? And righteousness to boot?

Yes, but not necessarily in that order. It's no mistake that one comes before the other. Peace, in fact, is a by-product of righteousness. You see, when we discipline ourselves into a right relationship with God, it means we eventually learn to rely on His ability to help us accomplish what we in our own flawed efforts often cannot. Only in that trust can we truly relax.

"Therefore," continues verses 12-13, "strengthen your feeble arms and weak knees. 'Make level paths for your feet,' so that the lame may not be disabled, but rather healed."

You'll notice that part of that last sentence is in quotations. That's because the Hebrews writer picked it up from another prolific pundit, King Solomon—also known as the wisest man in the Bible. What it indicates, loosely translated, is that if we, too, are wise, we'll muster our spiritual strength and set a route paved with practical, prayer-guided choices.

In other words, grab those spiritual bootstraps and get going. You'll feel better.

That's why a picture hanging in my home by artist Mary Englebreit so captures my heart. It depicts a happy-looking little fellow with a knapsack flung over his shoulder. He's just passed a crossroad marked by two street signs, one labeled "My Life," the other "No Longer an Option." Though the knapsack represents his total freedom to decide, the smile on his face indicates that he's picked the right path. He is headed toward life.

Near the end of Moses' life, God issued a similar challenge to the Israelites in Deuteronomy 30:19-20—"This day I call the heavens and the earth as witnesses against you that I have set before you life and death, blessings and curses. Now choose life, so that you and your children may live and that you may love the LORD your God, listen to his voice, and hold fast to him. For the LORD is your life, and he will give you many years in the land he swore to give to your fathers."

With Moses on his way out, it was time for the people to start making the tough choices for themselves. Whatever our unhealthful habits, it's time for us to do the same. Harkening back to our earlier scripture, Exodus 15:26, a couple of critical phrases leap out: "If you listen . . . if you pay attention." If we are to make long-term changes, we have to back up our mental choices with spiritual commitment. This means taking time to make the issues that affect our health a matter of prayer—even if we're afraid of what God might say—then allowing Him to help us alter our habits accordingly. To quote from one of my own books, *It All Comes Out in the Wash*, "Discipline works long-term only when it is spiritually motivated."

Bottom line, we have only one body. If we don't take time to care for it, it will eventually break down. Then we'll be taking a lot of time off. The tough truth is that while nobody lives forever, some of us are upping our expiration date.

"Wait a minute," someone might say. "What about God's sovereignty? Doesn't the Bible tell us that He knows the number of our days?"

Yes, and He also knows how some of the choices we're making are adversely affecting our outcome. Undoubtedly it's all calculated in. That's why if we don't take care of ourselves, God might send something unexpected along to get our attention.

Let me be quick to say that I certainly don't believe God makes us sick to punish us. But I do believe that ultimately our spiritual condition is more important to Him than our physical health. Thus, He may allow an illness or injury to slow us down long enough for Him to impart some solemn spiritual lessons. Amazing how quickly even a fleeting flu bug can put us on our backs, just long enough to get things into proper perspective. As Leviticus 26:35 symbolizes, "All the time that it lies desolate, the land will have the rest it did not have during the sabbaths you lived in it."

Sometimes this happens even during our sabbaticals, as was the case for author Janet McHenry. During a semester she took off from teaching school to write a book, her son had unexpected knee surgery, and she ended up caring for him. Lifting the machines he used for physical therapy several times a day, she badly blew a disk in her back. "For most of five weeks," Janet reported to our online writers' group, "I was in bed, unable to do much except pray. I spent a lot of time with God, and it was transformative in terms of becoming completely dependent on him."

The interesting outcome is that she also managed to finish her book. Do you suppose there could be a spiritual connection?

Here's one last point to ponder: besides affecting our organs, hearts, and arteries, how we care for our bodies also influences our outlook on life. Feeling unwell and out of control causes our thoughts to turn negative. This can lead to feelings of defeat, even downright depression, making it harder to achieve our highest potential. On the other hand, just knowing that we've begun the process of taking our health in hand almost automatically makes us feel better both physically and emotionally. No wonder Proverbs 17:22 says, "A cheerful heart is good medicine, but a crushed spirit dries up the bones."

Even in the face of a major health crisis, a positive attitude works wonders. Not long ago I read an interesting article on the benefits of humor in, of all things, cancer therapy. It quoted a review in *The Oncologist* magazine stating that not only is humor remedial in reducing stress and brightening your mood, but it can also boost pain tolerance. It's so successful, in fact, that some major hospitals have brought in clown comedians as part of their complementary therapy program. Lead author Richard T. Penson, clinical director of the Gillette Center for Gynecologic Oncology at Massachusetts General Hospital, puts it in this perspective: "Your outlook probably won't affect whether you live or die, but it does affect how you live with cancer"—and, I might add, a lot of other things.

Speaking of less stressful outlooks brings me back to our dear 1968 Olds Cutlass convertible. Truth is, it's a car that should have already seen its best days, except that the mechanic Jim bought it from had taken good care of it. Thankfully, despite my neglect, a few minor mechanical tweaks soon had it up and running again. Since then, it has provided us with many soft summer evenings of breeze-blowing-through-our-hair therapy, even a few chilly fall forays as we've bundled up and put down the top.

Just recently we took it on a short road trip culminating in a wonderful week of seaside solitude—one of the best, most restful times off we've taken since our official sabbatical. During those mellow moments, as God once again had our undivided attention, He gently reminded us how good it feels to take care of ourselves—and the car—while we can still enjoy both.

That, friends, is a huge, healthful step toward everyday Sabbath.

❖ 5 ❖
GIVE STRESS A REST

Anxiety weighs down the heart,
but a kind word cheers it up.
—Proverbs 12:25

As much as I hate to admit it, anxiety and I go a long way back. I was not quite twelve years old when I experienced my first awful attack. At that age, growing up in a loving and stable home, I had experienced little time or reason to suffer much real stress, let alone full-blown anxiety. Still, it didn't take long to discover the discernible difference and how quickly debilitating the latter can become. Without realizing it, I had just been enrolled in a lifelong class titled "Anxiety Awareness." My first assignment was to find the best formula for giving stress a rest.

For those fortunate enough not to know how an anxiety attack feels—or who just haven't put a label on it—let me briefly describe that initial introduction. It was the summer following sixth grade when a friend and I were planning a trip to the local amusement park. Like any kid, initially I was excited. Yet the closer time came to leave, the sicker I suddenly began to feel—not flu-sick, more like homesick. I remember thinking, *If I can just get home, I'll be okay.* So I hightailed it to my house a few blocks up the street.

I was right. By the time I got there, the feeling had passed. Unfortunately, it was only temporary. Through the rest of that summer and into my first year of junior high school, those unpredictable bouts of irrational, stomach-flipping fear followed me. Packed into a school assembly, I would become panicky. At home there were frightening times of feeling as if I couldn't catch my breath. Inexplicably, twilight often triggered a mood of extreme melancholy.

Finally my concerned mother took me to a doctor who ran a battery of tests, all inconclusive. Unable to pinpoint the cause, he resisted prescribing any medication. There was nothing else to do except put it into the Lord's hands and trust that I would soon be feeling better. That, in the end, is where I discovered anxiety's only reliable remedy.

About now someone is surely wondering, *Why in the world would a kid so young and otherwise healthy experience that kind of unexpected stress?* Sorry to tell you, but anxiety has no age limits. Looking back now, the cause was most likely the perfect pre-pubescent storm of combined physical and emotional changes swirling through my system. Besides battling havoc-wreaking hormones, I was also becoming more aware of the sometimes-scary world around me. Obviously a lot of things had been building up that I was unaware of until both my brain and body hit a tipping point.

Thankfully, by the middle of seventh grade not only had the baffling bouts subsided, but I had also gained an invaluable understanding on several levels. I learned that even while we're too busy to notice, life can be making some serious shifts, that our minds and bodies are finely balanced and connected, and that there are times when even the highest human wisdom fails us. Consequently, we can't and shouldn't wait until we've exhausted all other options before seeking God for His sustaining help and supernatural healing.

Pretty heavy stuff for a seventh-grader, huh? Yet all are precepts that have helped me retain emotional equilibrium over the years. Like everyone else on planet earth, it would not be the last time in my life I would have to deal with unexpected change—both physiological and otherwise. Hard as it was, I'm grateful to have learned those lessons early.

Believe it or not, experts say a certain amount of stress is actually good for us. Why? It motivates us into action. In fact, according to one article, when it comes to those occasional everyday elevations in stress, our bodies have an amazing natural ability to muster the energy to meet life's demands.[1] We know it as the fight-or-flight mechanism. Basically, when the need arises to act or react, our bodies release the stress hormones adrenaline and cortisol, our lungs take in more air, and heart rate and blood pressure rise, sending more oxygen to the muscles, even as blood vessels constrict to get more blood to the core of the body. All this adds up to a jolt of energy that enables us to hurry across a street, give a speech, meet a deadline, or run the bases.

But this works well only in bursts. To be healthful, these bursts should alternate with periods of rest. According to David Spiegel, the previously-quoted director of Stanford University's Center on Stress and Health, "Having periods when you turn down the stress response helps the operation of your immune system." Author and neuroimmuologist Esther Sternberg takes it a step further: "Taking a break can even boost levels of beneficial neurotransmitters and hormones that help you heal." That means both emotionally and physically.

Yet as we've already established, we rarely do it. No wonder, then, that we may achingly wake up some morning trying to remember when the last time was that we didn't feel weighed-down and weary—or worse, being suddenly surprised by a sweat-soaked panic attack. Both are clues that normal stress has morphed into something more potentially dangerous and debilitating.

So what exactly is *normal* stress? As we concluded in an earlier chapter, God never intended for stress to be normal. Yet that didn't keep it from cropping up. (Sprouting from an apple seed, perhaps?) That's why He gave us a book full of weed-trimming tools. Even so, each generation since Adam has seemed determined to try to function with what they deem acceptable levels. Problem is, the more complicated society becomes, the higher the bar gets set. By now one wonders if we haven't just thrown away the measuring stick. Surely it's the only explanation for why we've come to accept today's crazy-busy lifestyles as normal.

Let's see if we can put it back into somewhat proper perspective. For the most part, daily stress is connected to some specific, short-term situation. Whether unexpected, anticipated, or self-perpetuated, most of it is manageable if we'll only take the time to step back, recognize its source, and remedy it. Even in the case of stress that turns long-term, finding regular, healthful ways of releasing pent-up emotion is the key to keeping our cool. It's when we don't that things build up, anxiety rears its ugly head, and we're dealing with a whole different animal. According to experts, the key distinction between the two is that good stress feels exciting and energizing; the bad type feels scary and paralyzing.

One reason we sometimes have trouble diagnosing the subtle shift is that the causes of anxiety can be deep-rooted and illusive. Besides the common concerns most of us carry—many over circumstances out of our control—we all juggle a lot of other emotional luggage as well: guilt, regret, self-loathing, anger, resentment, and envy, just to name a few. The underlying reasons for these are too individually diverse to adequately address here. Suffice it to say, the longer we live, the more things we all experience that evoke and establish these emotions. No wonder we find ourselves wobbling under the weight of stress that we may not even understand.

Add to that an overt, sometimes self-imposed sense of responsibility, and whump! We're soon sitting smack in the middle of an overgrown weed patch of worry. And what often inhabits high grass? Snakes! Suddenly stress has propelled us into the path of some poisonous spiritual consequences.

One of the main spiritual battles many of us fight is fear—much of it unfounded. In fact, statistics tell us that ninety percent of the things we worry about never happen. Yet like a stray cat, we can't seem to stop feeding them. Soon some have grown to paranoid proportions. For many people, just watching the evening news is enough to put our fear into high gear. Speaking for myself, I decided a long time ago that there is a fine line between being informed and frightened. When it comes to giving stress a rest, may I suggest avoiding—or at least limiting—the television shows, news segments, and online litanies that foster fear. Since the reporting of bad news so far outweighs the good, we must take it upon ourselves to bring balance. "Resist the devil," says James 4:7, "and he will flee from you." (See also 1 Peter 5:6-11.)

Please understand, however, that I'm not saying we shouldn't be informed about current events—just that we need not subject ourselves to repeated exposure to sordid and disgusting details. Each of us must know our his or her emotional limits.

By doing so, we might also be doing our kids a favor. If the circumstances during my growing-up years contributed to anxiety, imagine how compounded it is for this generation living in a mostly uncensored society where every imaginable, horrible thing is being played out in our living rooms and on social media. Because children now seem to mature so much earlier physically, we sometimes forget how emotionally immature and stress-sensitive they still are. Thus, we may tend not to shield them from media exposure as much as we should. Let's not forget, either, the largest and most potentially dangerous challenge of all: monitoring and limiting what they are viewing online.

Another thing we must monitor is how we often allow our own stress to spill over, not to mention allowing ourselves to be splashed on by others. This happens so often that there's now a name for it: "stresscalation." Though the original term was coined by Ruth Daily Graninger in a 1992 article for the *American Journal of Nursing* to describe how we exacerbate our own stress through such things as obsessive thinking, worry over the future, procrastination, and perfectionism, it can also be used to describe the way stress can be passed on to others.

There's no doubt that personality plays a part in how stress affects us. My husband, for instance, is not a naturally fearful person. Unlike me, he doesn't get onto an airplane already expecting the worst to happen. The way his brain works, he's already miles ahead mentally contemplating what we have to do upon arrival even as I'm settling white-knuckled into my seat. Truth is, in almost every case, we process stress very differently.

Admittedly, since I'm a creative person, much of my stress is the result of an imagination that is always in overdrive—both a blessing and a curse. It's something I have to continually commit to the Lord. It also helps to remind myself what Dan Zadra, founder of Compendium—one of the nation's foremost creators of inspiring books and gifts—once said: "Worry is a misuse of imagination."

Another personality flaw that can rob us of rest is perfectionism. How well I remember when I was working feverishly to finish my first book, *Prodigal in the Parsonage*—a book of encouragement for those in ministry dealing with children who have rejected faith. Chronicling our own painful journey with our oldest son, it was an emotional project, to say the least. Add to that the pressure every aspiring author feels to produce something of redeeming value to the reader. Already past my deadline, I finally came to the last chapter but just wasn't finding a satisfactory way to finish. The more I tried to tweak it, the more frustrated I became.

One evening, hoping to help, my husband stood behind me at the computer. "It sounds good to me, honey. Just stop and send it off."

My sharper-than-intended response was fraught with frustration. "I would if I could, Jim, but I'm just not happy with it!"

What he probably wanted to say—hands up in a position of surrender—was "Okay, Judi. Just step away from the computer, and no one will get hurt!" Instead, knowing me well, he took the wiser way out and slipped silently back to watching television.

What I've since come to realize is how my own self-imposed perfectionism, warring with an overdue deadline, was actually working against me, eventually taking the form of writer's block. Finally I had no choice but to temporarily put the project aside until, with fresh eyes, I was able to make the satisfactory changes. Ironically, in the end it was my husband who gave me a great concluding illustration. If only I had taken time to listen sooner.

"The time to relax," according to American journalist Sydney J. Harris, "is when you don't have time for it." If we don't, there comes a point at which we lose complete perspective. Backing away and letting any project or situation settle almost always results in a better end product than any amount of continued tweaking—or nagging, or yelling.

As in my early experience, there may be times when we truly don't know what is causing our anxiety. As hard as it is to admit, due to hormonal fluctuations women really are more predisposed to stress than men. Add to that our maternal, nurturing nature that often causes us to take the stress of others on top of our own. What I've learned to employ is my "Wait Three Days" theory. When you sense that stress may be in any way related to a change in body chemistry or irrational reasoning, it's a good idea to delay if possible any personal confrontations or major decisions until things level out a little.

Of course, there are other kinds of chemical imbalances that are no respecter of gender or age. Take for instance John, a deacon at one of our former churches who began to experience severe bouts of nervousness and depression. After months of testing, it was finally determined that he was deficient in a certain brain enzyme that was then successfully treated with medication. Let me be quick to say this was different from those who suffer from actual mind-altering diseases such as bipolar disorder. These fall into a much more dangerous category that require carefully monitored treatment.

Our bodies are finely tuned instruments, ones that should move daily in rhythm with the Great Conductor. Thank goodness He is also the Great Creator and understands better than anyone on earth what is going on in our minds and bodies. That's all the more reason we should simply stop at the first sign of stress and seek His infinite wisdom in pursuing the best course of action in every situation.

Whatever the things are that we anguish over, whether real or imagined, short-term or long, they serve no positive purpose. Rather, they are a trick our ancient enemy uses to divert our eyes onto circumstances and away from God. Not only do they steal our present joy, they also keep us from moving forward. As great nineteenth-century preacher Charles Spurgeon said, "Anxiety does not empty tomorrow of its sorrows but only empties today of its strength." Whether stress becomes a positive driver or a negative drainer depends on how we choose to respond.

There's only one way to break the cycle of stress: stop attempting to figure things out yourself, and admit that you need help. Too often we just keep trudging on, hoping that if we ignore it long enough it will go away. That's why, unfortunately, it often takes something drastic to bring us to the breaking point.

It might make us feel better to know that we're in good biblical company. We've already seen how driving all those discontented Israelites around the desert caused Moses no small stress. At Mt. Sinai we even watched him experience a major meltdown. Still, he trod on, trying his best to keep the God-appointed plates spinning. Overall, however, things were not going well.

In fact, it was not long after the Mt. Sinai incident that God got so fed up with the whole stiff-necked situation that He threatened something He had never done before: to let the Israelites go it alone. Screech! That not only got Moses' attention but also brought the entire mopey mob to a complete halt.

Here, summarily, is how Exodus 33:1-2 records it. Following a little plague of idol-induced punishment, God had again given the group a go-ahead to the land of milk and honey that He had promised their descendants. He even agreed to send an angel before them to banish the bad guys. As far as the Israelites could tell, it was business as usual—another day, another desert. Then in verse 3 God drops the bombshell: "But I will not go with you, because you are a stiff-necked people and I might destroy you on the way."

What?

Whether or not Moses had a camel, this was the final back-breaking straw. Skipping down to verse 12, the passage tells how he headed straight to the tent of meeting to have a little talk with the Lord. There he did what all of us tend to do when stress hits a high note. First we whine; then we look for someone else to blame it all on. In Moses' case, it was God. Let's listen in.

Moses said to the LORD, "You have been telling me, 'Lead these people,' but you have not let me know whom you will send with me. You have said, 'I know you by name and you have found favor with me.' If you are pleased with me, teach me your ways so I may know you and continue to find favor with you. Remember that this nation is your people" (*Exodus 33:12-13*).

Picture it with me. Arms out, palms turned beseechingly up, here's how I interpret Moses' little tirade: "It's not fair, Lord! Why me? This whole Exodus thing was your idea, but so far you haven't given me much help. Why you ever liked me enough to give me this job I'll never know [heavy sigh], but since you do, could you at least supply a little extra spiritual insight so I'll know how to stay in your good graces? Oh, and may I remind you, these are *your* people."

In case you've ever had a similar conversation with God, here are two nice things to know. First, unlike us, He never forgets who's in charge. Second, He's really good at listening between the lines. Consequently, what He heard Moses acknowledging were three things: "I'm tired. I can't do this by myself anymore. I need help."

That's all God wanted to hear. Finally, in verse 14, come the words that in the midst of any stressful situation—especially when it involves people we're agonizing over—give us hope.

"The LORD replied, 'My Presence will go with you, and I will give you rest.'"

Praise-a-lujah! Even in the middle of a desert-induced melt-down, God's presence always provides us with a place of rest.

Still, just to confirm that the deal was sealed, Moses submits one more statement: "If your Presence does not go with us, do not send us up from here" (verse 15). In other words, "I'm just telling you, Lord—if you don't go with us, we're not taking one more step." Finally Moses was more than ready to permanently release the balance of power to its rightful owner.

Skipping to verse 17, we read God's reassurance. "And the LORD said to Moses, 'I will do the very thing you have asked, because I am pleased with you and I know you by name.'"

Dear pressure-prone pilgrim—the next time someone steps on your last nerve and you finally realize that doing life on your own has brought you to the end of your strength and resources, those are words to remember: *God—knows—your—name.* Despite your faults and failings, despite your ineffective attempts to put your own life in order, despite the pressure others contribute to your life, He hasn't forgotten you or left you. Without going through a lot of spiritual gymnastics, all you have to do is ask for help, and His presence is right there with you. As Moses learned, all it takes is a simple shift of responsibility, and instantly, you've found the only real way to give stress a rest. You must leave it with the Lord.

The good news is that just as God gave Joshua to Moses as a spiritual support, he sends others alongside to help you. Let me say here how thankful I am for committed Christian counselors who pursue professional training in all areas of stress and life management. We should never hesitate to seek their help—the sooner the better.

Most important, of course, God has given us the greatest helper of all. His name is Jesus, which, in fact, in Hebrew is *Yeshua*—a variation of Joshua. Yet of all the many biblical names for Jesus, the one I love most and fits best here is the one prophesied by the angel to his mother, Mary: Immanuel—which according to Matthew 1:23 means "God with us."

This chapter's theme scripture, Proverbs 12:25, says it all: "Anxiety weighs down the heart, but a kind word cheers it up."

And what are some good words for today and every day? We have a Bible full of them. For "sabbatitude" starters, listen to Jesus' own words found in Matthew 11:28-30: "Come to me, all you who are weary and burdened, and I will give you rest. Take my yoke upon you and learn from me, for I am gentle and humble in heart, and you will find rest for your souls. For my yoke is easy and my burden is light."

Seems ironic, doesn't it, that the only way we let go of our weary weight is by hanging His harness on us. Yet, though other yokes could be considered shackles, in this case it's a coupling. Jesus shares it with us—that's why it's easy and light. Of course, in order to build spiritual muscle and stamina, we must bear some weight. But as long as we keep the Lord on the other side He will make sure our burdens stay in balance. Then we can say with the writer of Psalm 68:19, "Praise be to the Lord, to God our Savior, who daily bears our burdens."

There's another good word: *daily.*

In Matthew 6:25-34, speaking to His disciples, Jesus uses two familiar examples to put our problems in perspective even as He covers every concern we could possibly conjure:

> Therefore I tell you do not worry about your life, what you will eat or drink; or about your body, what you will wear. Is not life more important than food, and the body more important than clothes? Look at the birds of the air;

they do not sow or reap or store away in barns, and yet your heavenly Father feeds them. Are you not much more valuable than they? Can any one of you by worrying add a single hour to your life?

And why do you worry about clothes? See how the flowers of the field grow. They do not labor or spin. Yet I tell you that not even Solomon in all his splendor was dressed like one of these. If that is how God clothes the grass of the field, which is here today and tomorrow is thrown into the fire, will he not much more clothe you—you of little faith? So do not worry, saying, "What shall we eat?" or "What shall we drink?" or "What shall we wear?" For the pagans run after all these things, and your heavenly Father knows that you need them. But seek first his kingdom and his righteousness, and all these things will be given to you as well. Therefore do not worry about tomorrow, for tomorrow will worry about itself. Each day has enough trouble of its own.

It was author Henry Ward Beecher who said, "Every tomorrow has two handles. We can take hold of it with the handle of anxiety or the handle of faith." Surely this is a choice we all have to make over and over. Yet every leap of faith is also a spring toward this next "sabbatitude": that each time we choose to trust God, we open a door over whose threshold we can hand our stress to its rightful owner, exchanging it for wisdom, direction, and rest.

❖ 6 ❖

CHILD'S PLAY

*Through the praise of children and infants you have
established a stronghold against your enemies,
to silence the foe and the avenger.*

—Psalm 8:2

"I like your shoes."

The words, spoken by a little gray-haired lady standing behind me in the grocery line, caught me off guard. I had made one of those late-in-the-day dashes to the store and at the moment was more focused on getting home to fix dinner than on conversation or couture. Now, pulled from my preoccupation, I looked down at the pair of flats I was wearing that though casual were covered entirely in silver sequins. No surprise she had noticed them.

"Thanks," I said. Then suddenly self-conscious by this unexpected exposure of my fancy footwear, I couldn't seem to stop myself from offering further explanation. "I actually planned on buying a plainer version," I babbled on, "but these were the only ones they had in my size."

A mischievous smile rejuvenated her wrinkled face. "Oh, no, honey. You should *always* pick the ones with sparkles."

That's when I knew. The gray hair was merely a clever cover-up. Behind me was an incognito kid, someone young at heart who still embraces the joy of doing something silly and spontaneous.

Don't you love it when someone—particularly an older person—has such a capricious outlook on life? Undoubtedly it's because at that age he or she has finally managed to sort out what is really important in life and how little time is left to enjoy it. The older I get, the clearer it's becoming: you go around only once and need to make the most of it.

Granted, reaching those golden years also means—if we work it right—having freedom from a few of the responsibilities that keep the rest of the world running, like full-time jobs, maintaining homes, and raising children. Undoubtedly a lot of us long for that treasured time when we finally have more flexibility. Of course, age has its own set of stresses. Still, even as we're paying today's unavoidable dues, we might want to reflect for a moment on that word *running*. As Carl Honore, author of *In Praise of Slowness,* reminds us, "Most people are running through their lives instead of living them."[1] Surely there's space in there somewhere for not only spontaneity but also sparkles.

The reality is that we have no guarantee—especially if we insist on maintaining these marathon lifestyles—whether we'll even get to the golden years or how long our health will permit us to hang around and enjoy them. That's why we need to heed the grocery store lady's advice and look for every opportunity to lighten up a little. Come to think of it, maybe that's the best guarantee we have.

In case you consider the concept of fun somewhat sparse in God's vocabulary, let me share yet another little Sabbath insight. Even though God made Sabbath rest a holy commandment, he established it around times of celebration. Could it be that, like every good parent, God knew the best way to entrench tradition and teach His children the true underlying meaning was to make it more enjoyable? Why else would so many Jewish feasts and festivals be associated with the Sabbath, and vice versa?

In Leviticus 23 we find a comprehensive list and description of these. It includes Passover, the LORD's Festival of Unleavened Bread, Firstfruits, Weeks, Trumpets, and Tabernacles. In addition was the Day of Atonement, which unlike the others required a time of fasting. Still, they all involved group gatherings that emphasized times of reflection, restoration, and celebration focusing on God's protection, provision, goodness, new way of life, joy, thanksgiving, harvest bounty, atonement, salvation, and preservation. All promoted an outlook of peace, hope, and happiness—not a bad thing to take time out for while you're wandering in the wilderness.

Most also involved food, which makes it tempting to imagine that they might have been precursors to our present-day church potlucks. Fact is, though these are all distinctive Jewish holidays linked to specific Old Testament times and teachings, some bear similarities to other cultures' holidays or traditions. The Feast of Firstfruits, for instance, somewhat resembles the American holiday of Thanksgiving in that they were both established to celebrate completion of the harvest's hard work, as well as a time of thankfulness to God for His bountiful provision. In my way of thinking, anything involving food and fellowship has to be fun.

The Feast of Tabernacles could strike a chord with anyone who has ever attended a rustic church retreat or old-fashioned camp meeting, since during this time the Israelites were ordered to live in booths, or tents. This was probably not too exciting for the group who had just graduated from those dusty dwellings but important for future generations who needed to be reminded of the hardships as well as God's protection and guidance as the Israelites fled to the Promised Land. It served as an opportunity for Israel to renew its commitment and trust in His continued care.

This reminds me of a time not long ago when Jim and I took two of our grandkids to a church camp that met in the beautiful but remote northern California redwoods, and all the attendees stayed in either cabins or RVs. Following the morning meeting, everyone was free to explore the surroundings, swim in a nearby mountain stream, or just kick back. In the evening we all met in a rough-hewn tabernacle for an unhurried time of singing and sharing God's Word.

For Jim and me it was a nostalgia trip, not only reliving our own youthful church camp experiences but also recalling the more simple but sincere style of worship that had defined our early religious upbringing. For our grandkids, it was the first time they had been exposed to the rural roots of their spiritual heritage. In that relaxed and rustic atmosphere, it was amazingly easy for us to regress to the level of our grands and do a little splashing and exploring ourselves—all in all, a great time of building both foundations and memories together. Free, I might add, from television, video games, and cell phones.

Back to those previously mentioned Jewish celebrations, for anyone who might enjoy a delightfully in-depth description I recommend checking out a book recently written by Joyce Meyers. Titled *Eat the Cookie . . . Buy the Shoes*, it focuses on bringing guilt-free balance into life. In it she writes, "The Sabbath was a day when people would remember and celebrate all that He [God] had done for them and what He had created. It was a time of reflection, restoration, and celebration."[2]

Imagine how much more enjoyable our own Sabbath services might be if we saw them as celebrations rather than obligations. I've always believed church should be a place to which we enjoy going, a place where we can leave our cares outside the doors in joyful anticipation of all that awaits us within. That's why they call it a "sanctuary." Viewing it as such might help us truly understand what King David meant when he wrote Psalm 122:1—"I rejoiced with those who said to me, 'Let us go to the house of the LORD.'"

It's most likely those who don't see it that way may neglect going and miss a big blessing. As one reviewer of Mark Buchanan's book, *The Rest of God*, wrote, "God commanded us to keep [the Sabbath], knowing we might neglect it. And when we neglect it, we lose not only His rest but the joy of knowing more of the God who gives us that rest. This festive day of refreshment and playfulness releases us from the tyranny of busy schedules and agendas and fills us with wholeness and freedom."[3]

One of the things I miss most now that Jim and I no longer serve as pastors of a local congregation is behind-the-scenes participation in planning the church's seasonal celebrations. Particularly Easter, Thanksgiving, and Christmas were always fun, warm times of reflection, reverence, and fellowship with our children and church family. Of course, we still enjoy participating from the pew, and every church gathering provides us a wonderful time of worshiping the Lord. Yet it's the commemoration of Christ's birth and resurrection that still stand out as the main reminders of why we should be celebrating every single day. Jesus truly is the reason for *every* season.

I believe many will agree that the highlights of these special occasions are always the children's programs. Why is that? Basically because you never know what the little rascals will do or say. Their uninhibited joy and excitement are contagious. Seen through the eyes of a child, every celebration takes on a delightfully fresh dimension. Even non-Christian family members come without coercion just to experience the enjoyment. It's no wonder that often in that atmosphere the seemingly hardest of hearts are won over. Somehow any anti-spiritual argument seems futile against the faith shining in those innocent, enthusiastic faces.

As Psalm 8:2, the theme scripture for this chapter, states, "Through the praise of children and infants you have established a stronghold against your enemies, to silence the foe and the avenger." The *Message* version makes it even plainer: "Nursing infants gurgle choruses about you; toddlers shout the songs that drown out enemy talk and silence atheist babble." The significance of this scripture is emphasized in Matthew 21:16 when—following His ride into Jerusalem surrounded by children shouting, "Hosanna to the Son of David!"—Jesus quotes it to the indignant scribes and teachers.

It makes sense, then, that recapturing some of the child-ike delight we all experienced before the cares and inhibitions of life took over might go a long way toward silencing our own ancient enemy's trash talk—that same scaly serpent who stole Adam and Eve's innocence and still strives to rob us of fellowship with our Heavenly Father.

Of course, we're not talking about being childlike in the sense of simpleminded, acting immaturely, or even experiencing a "second childhood," which sometimes carries the connotation of a diminished mentality. We're simply speaking of finding ways to accept, embrace, and relish the simple and serendipitous things in life that provide a temporary reprieve from the pressure and turn our hearts toward God. "Truly I tell you," Jesus directed the disciples in Luke 18:17, "anyone who will not receive the kingdom of God like a little child will never enter it." A childlike spirit truly is the key to the Kingdom.

The problem for some of us is that we've forgotten what it is like to be a kid. Let's see if we can recall a few things that might still be translatable.

If memory serves, the two things that took up a major part of our day as young children were play and naps. Even when we entered kindergarten and took our first step toward a more structured environment, the teachers attempted to make learning fun by interspersing it with games, art, and fun physical activities. A rug and blanket were also requisite for use during regular rest times.

I realize that as adults we are not all fortunate enough to have jobs that allow us to incorporate creative interests or keep a cot in the corner. But I believe we can all look for ways to balance work with a little levity and leisure.

Earlier this year I found a great illustration for this while walking the dog in our local park. I spotted an abandoned bird's nest in the bare branches of a tree. As I came closer, a flash of bright blue caught my eye. To my delight, woven into the nest was a shiny cerulean ribbon undoubtedly left over from some child's open-air party. Think about it. If even a bird chooses to so brighten its nest, surely we can find ways to weave color into our prickly worlds as well.

Some of us might even consider trading in a truly tedious job, perhaps by taking advantage of an opportunity to train for something that better suits our abilities and interests, something we might even find—dare I say it?—enjoyable. Even if it necessitates a cut in pay, the personal fulfillment could be enough to compensate.

That brings us back to another common childhood trait: not being afraid to try anything. After all, when you ask a kindergarten class who can draw, most raise their hands. They don't impose self-defeating expectations or limitations on themselves. Nor do they have any hang-ups when it comes to being satisfied with a job well done, rather than, as some adults do, berating themselves for not doing it differently or better.

At the very least, we should make time in our off-hours to do something just for the sheer enjoyment of it—painting, drama, or crafting, perhaps. Consider trying, say, a Zumba class instead of the usual exercise routine. And how about playing an instrument? Many of us took music lessons as children, then gave it up when life got too hectic—yet secretly we wish we had stayed with it. News flash! It's never too late to re-learn something you once loved. Check out the adult education classes at your local community center or college.

Then there is the matter of restful rejuvenation. Ever notice how a kid can conk out almost anywhere? Though we already suggested some nocturnal sleep-inducing remedies in a previous chapter, this is different. When is the last time you allowed yourself the luxury of snatching a short snooze during the day—or, for that matter, a long nap?

As for drifting dreamily off to sleep at night without some worry weighing heavy on our hearts, perhaps it would help if we reinstituted another regular childhood ritual: bedtime prayers.

How many remember this one?

Now I lay me down to sleep;
I pray the Lord my soul to keep.
If I should die before I wake,
I pray the Lord my soul to take.

Though, to some, that last part might seem a little scary, I don't remember ever being concerned about it as a child, especially since it was usually followed by "God, bless Mommy, Daddy, Aunt Myrtle," and so on. Somehow it seemed that once prayers were said, we could sleep soundly, knowing all the bases had been covered.

But then children are naturally a lot more trusting than adults. Hardly ever do they hesitate to ask for what they want, never doubting that they will get it. Nor do they yet have any delusions of grandeur or prideful preconceived ideas. For the most part, children do what they enjoy and resist what is forced on them or unrealistically expected of them. These are acquired adult traits.

So ask yourself, *How long since I bounced into bed believing that all is well with the world*—or even if it isn't, that God is serving as night watchman? Amazing how a simple bedtime prayer still serves as a great way of settling our minds and bodies before slipping into sleep. It brings to mind the familiar phrase "slept like a baby" which for me paints a mental picture of being so bundled in trust that we're overtaken by warmth, eyelids soon growing too heavy to hold open.

That's undoubtedly why Jesus loved children and rebuked the disciples for turning them away. They were innocent and unspoiled. Approaching Him without fear, they expected to be loved and accepted. It was He who said in Matthew 18:3-4: "Truly I tell you, unless you change and become like little children, you will never enter the kingdom of heaven. Therefore, whoever takes the lowly position of this child is the greatest in the kingdom of heaven."

Children have no hesitation believing what they cannot see, a confidence we should incorporate more often, especially when we pray. Nor do they require a lot to be happy. Ever notice how a kid will often play with the box as much as the gift that came in it? Likewise, we need to retrain ourselves to focus on the simpler pleasures in life.

Years ago when we lived in Anchorage, Alaska, we experienced winters that were notoriously cold and long, with very few daylight hours. For some people it could be depressing. Still, there was nothing more beautiful than the days when the sun came out, releasing a million small sparkles onto the snow. Those were the days I sometimes took the opportunity to sit by a sunny window and feel the reflected heat. If at home, I might grab a pillow and just lie on the floor near our sliding glass door. What is it about that radiating warmth that stops us in our tracks and brings a sense of contentment not only to our bodies but also to our souls?

Of course, you don't have to live in Alaska to experience the occasional need for defrosting, especially in the emotional or spiritual department. It's then we should take time to just sit in the presence of the Son, allowing Him to cast His warmth on our souls.

Another thing I remember spending a lot of time doing as a child was reading with an abandon than seems harder to achieve now as an adult. I love the following word picture painted by author George Howe Colt in the pages of one of my favorite books, *The Big House: A Century in the Life of an American Summer Home*. Reflecting on his childhood love for reading, especially on a rainy afternoon, he writes,

> Lying on my stomach, I saw nothing but the book and the patch of blue bedspread that framed it. I was dimly aware of the ship's clock chiming, a car crackling up the driveway, the chandelier's shadow lengthening across the ceiling, and I had the strange sensation that although I was holding this small rectangle of cloth and paper in my hands, it was really holding me.
>
> My body lay there for hours, while my mind walked the cobblestone streets of London or the dusty canyons of Nevada. And then I would turn the last page and suddenly realize that I wasn't in the Emerald City but here in the living room of the Big House.[4]

How rarely we adults give in to the guiltless freedom of whiling away an entire afternoon reading! Even briefly tucking into a book, newspaper, or magazine can offer a delicious diversion, having the capacity in a few short moments to take us to an entirely different place and time. It's like a vacation for your mind without leaving home. Perhaps it would pay—considering how often we hurry only to find ourselves waiting in lines, at the doctor's office, chauffeuring our family members, and so on—to develop the habit of carrying our current favorite reading material along in order to fill those otherwise empty moments with enjoyment. Personally I read myself to sleep each night. It's like my much-anticipated dessert at the end of the day.

When it comes to real vacations, kids don't care whether they take a trip around the world or just to the local Dairy Queen. Yet as adults we often regard a true getaway as something that requires months of planning and may result in years of paying off. Perhaps that's why some never materialize—or we end up being disappointed when the long-anticipated event doesn't match our overinflated expectations. I'm not telling anyone to cancel his or her dream vacation—I'm suggesting that less-complicated but more easily, evenly dispersed times of getaway and recreation might provide equal benefits.

Find something close to home—maybe a car show or museum. Better yet, don't even leave home. Instead, some starry summer night stretch a white sheet on the fence, rent or borrow a digital projector, and show your own outdoor movie complete with popcorn. Or when the winter wind whistles outside, lay out a picnic in front of the fireplace. I guarantee the kids will love it.

Another thing kids do is laugh a lot, often at the most ridiculous things. In fact, statistics tell us that kids laugh four hundred times a day as compared to fifteen times for adults. Does that mean we outgrow our sense of humor? More likely, we are just too preoccupied to practice it—especially in the small things. Or worse, we're so sophisticated we won't give in to a good guffaw. When's the last time some silly thing struck you so funny that you laughed until you cried or got you so tickled it resulted in a startling nose snort or two?

Psychologists say the best stress-reduction techniques are those that relax your muscles or clear concern from your mind. A good laugh does both. So next time something triggers a giggle, give in to the impulse. Not only will it do you good—it could be contagious.

Perhaps for some of us childhood didn't leave a lot to laugh about. If so, I can't think of a better reason to allow ourselves some long-overdue enjoyment. As author Tom Robbins reminds us, "It's never too late to have a happy childhood."

In reality, the only reason many of us enjoyed carefree childhoods was that we had parents we could trust to take care of all the important stuff, freeing us to play, grow, and just *be*. How wonderful it is to know that whatever our growing-up experience might have been, whatever our adult responsibilities currently are, we have a Heavenly Father to whom we can still hand the heavy stuff! In 1 Peter 5:7 we're encouraged to—"Cast all your anxiety on him because he cares for you." The God who created us in the beginning is all about renewal, rebirth, and recapturing what we may have missed. He is the God of not only second chances but also of second childhoods.

Of course, the times inevitably come to all of us when we realize that life cannot always be fun and games. It's then, according to the late author Calvin Miller, our playful nature can serve as a serious respite. "We play," I once heard him state, "while we wait for insights and in the fearful moments of our lives."

As with much of Miller's brilliant writings, it took me a while to digest that. The first part was easier to understand than the last. As we've already discussed, finding some sort of mental diversion is usually the best way for inspiration, insights, and solutions to surface. But the idea of playing in the fearful moments seems somehow contradictory.

Then I remembered one of the most difficult days of my life: the day my mother died. In the moments immediately following, with nothing yet for our grieving family to do, we were at loose ends—especially my dad, who had just lost the person with whom he had spent the last sixty-two years of his life. The prospect of going on alone must, at that moment, have been too frightening for him to comprehend.

So we did the only thing that seemed reasonable. We headed to a nearby Chinese restaurant for lunch—a buffet, which had long been one of my father's favorites. At the time, I remember it seemed surreal that any of us could eat, but looking back now I see that was exactly what we needed to do. It was something that if not fun was familiar, something that made us feel as if life might actually go on as usual—though we all knew it wouldn't. Somehow that small pivotal act provided us with the equilibrium to accept reality and move on.

Thinking of my mother, I can tell you this. She would have had no problem with that. She was a fun-loving lady who always made life happier for those around her, believing that the only thing worse than getting old is *acting* old.

This brings me to one last story about yet another lady who had a great impact on our lives, someone my husband and I became acquainted with when we came to pastor the church she attended. Then in her sixties, Shirley Hawkins was one of the most young-at-heart people I've ever known. She was one of those people whose laugh was infectious and frequent, who exuded a true joy of living.

Fact is, Shirley was a fun magnet—crazy things were always happening to her. I recall the time she and some friends were sitting in a restaurant and a bug fell into her bleached-blond bouffant. Instead of freaking out, she took it in stride and soon had everyone around her laughing. Her playful personality never wanted anyone to miss out on anything.

Growing up in Utah, Shirley was raised Mormon and didn't embrace a personal relationship with Christ until much later in life. When she did, her generous spirit and love for life just naturally transferred over. She exuded a childlike faith and spirit that simply couldn't see the bad in people. Consequently, she had been taken advantage of a few times but never became bitter. She simply had no time for anything that made life less enjoyable.

Reading this, one might conclude that she had a life devoid of stress or hardship. But as we became better acquainted with Shirley, we discovered a different story. Not only had she outlived three husbands, but she was never able to have children. As an only child herself, her family, with the exception of one cousin, was deceased. Though she had plenty of reason to pity herself, we never saw her succumb.

Even after Jim and I moved on in ministry, we stayed in touch with Shirley, managing for many years to keep an annual lunch date. If we thought we were doing her a favor by getting her out and about, it always proved the other way around. We never left without feeling lighter somehow, less bogged down in our circumstances.

Last year we got word from a mutual friend that Shirley was in a nursing home, near death due to age-related complications from pneumonia. The next day I went to visit her, not knowing what to expect. In true form, she roused enough to smile and sing with me a few of the old hymns she loved so dearly.

When Shirley passed away, true to his longstanding promise, my husband helped conduct her memorial service. As those in attendance recounted story after story, there was far more laughter than tears—an amazing celebration of a life well and joyfully lived. Her current pastor even suggested we collaborate on a book titled *Shirley, You Jest*. If our fun-loving friend is any example, a sunny outlook on life could also contribute to a long one. Shirley was ninety-three years old.

As for me, ever since my chance encounter with the little lady at the grocery store, I've made it a point to put more sparkles in life. One way I keep my inner kid alive is by doing what I call "Camp Gramma" with my grandkids every year. This involves planning fun activities intermingled with Bible stories and spiritual lessons. I don't know who has more fun—me or the kids. Equally fun was the book I wrote titled *Camp Gramma*, which is full of experiences and encouragement for other grandparents.[5]

And if you're wondering about my sequined shoes, you might smile to know that I still wear them—yes, even to the grocery store—for no other reason than they make me happy. Especially on the days that are harried and hurried, we need all the happiness we can get.

So join me, people! Life is too short to always take the safe and serious route. Let's lace up our sequined sneakers, and together, we'll take another super-sparkly step toward "sabbatitude."

❖ 7 ❖

RESTFUL RELATIONSHIPS

Whoever refreshes others will be refreshed.
—Proverbs 11:25

"The quality of our lives," stated my pastor during a recent sermon, "is determined by the quality of our relationships." Nothing could be truer. Good friends and loving family are like islands in the fast-moving streams of life. They provide a place where we can temporarily dock from our duties, shuck off our shoes, and wiggle our toes in the warm sand of companionship. I call them "featherbed friends," because they provide us with a soft place to land. How restoring it can be when we make room in our lives for those who support, encourage, and lift our spirits!

Unfortunately, not every relationship will be as restful. We all know those as well who, whether consciously or unconsciously, drain us dry if we let them. Somehow in our search for more respites during the daily rigors, we must learn to differentiate between the two, investing more time in the first even as we learn to limit or, in some cases, eliminate the latter.

The reality is that there will be only a few choice comrades throughout a lifetime who truly care and understand unconditionally enough to stay the course. I can tell you from experience that you can be the most popular person on the block—

one with a Facebook full of friends—but very few real and restful ones. Likewise, you can spend your life constantly surrounded with people and still end up lonely if you don't take time to cultivate the keepers and cull out the seepers.

Take Moses, for instance. He was one in a million—literally. Toward the end of his life the Israelites had multiplied like—to use their leader's own lingo—"the stars in the sky." There were so many he finally had to divide them into tribes and assign overseers. I have occasionally thought if it hadn't been for all those Israelites, Moses might have enjoyed a nice, long vacation. Because of them, it was anything but. Thank goodness, God gave him a few good friends. Consider the following three.

First there was his brother Aaron, who after a shaky start at the bottom of Mt. Sinai became a solid spiritual overseer, one who despite his shortcomings had stayed at Moses' side from the very beginning.

Then there was Hur (no relation to Ben), whose most famous mention was in Exodus 17:12-13. There during Israel's first fierce battle, he, along with Aaron, found Moses a stone to sit on; then each held up one of his weary, weakening hands—a one-time-only requisite to ensure that the Israelites won.

That particular battle also provided our first introduction to Joshua, who "overcame the Amalekite army with the sword." After proving himself in battle, Joshua became Moses' trusted aide and apprentice—one who, unlike others, is never recorded in Scripture as questioning Moses' leadership or authority. Not only did he fight for Moses—he fed from Him. No wonder God ultimately appointed him successor.

To me these represent the three most common friendship categories: the faithful few who sometimes span a lifetime, those who support us through short but significant seasons, and the ones who become our mutual mentors as we carry out a common legacy.

By now some may be wondering if finding these feather-bed buddies might prove more challenging than it seems. Yet I believe there are ways we can determine which relationships warrant nurturing and which do not, thus saving ourselves a lot of stress in the process. Let's start with the beginning stages.

Most of us have the tendency to base any potential pal-ship on an initial "clicking" of personalities. If there is something we immediately like about or identify with a person, we may entertain the idea of becoming better acquainted. There will also be times when we're tossed together with those with whom we seem to share little in common, in which case we might quickly consider them as crummy candidates.

My experience is this: don't be too hasty in embracing or dismissing people simply on the basis of face value. In both cases, what we see is not always what we get. We should make commitments carefully, being willing to invest enough time to make sure they are not only successful but also restful.

Consider Jesus' disciples. They came from a variety of backgrounds—a few fishermen, a tax collector, a political zealot, a doubter, and, unbeknownst to all but Jesus, an untrustworthy traitor. The fishermen were the only ones with anything in common and frankly didn't always get along that well. On more than one occasion, all the disciples competed with and irritated each other.

Eventually, though—thanks to a few well-placed beatitudes from the Master—they learned to appreciate each other's strengths and bolster their weaknesses. Starting with a common call they all but one ended up supporting and encouraging each other to the Cross and beyond. It was their fire-forged unity that laid the foundation for the Early Church. In truth some of the deepest, most restful and resilient friendships are the ones we grow into, learning over a period of time not only to appreciate each other's qualities but also to overlook a few faults and failures.

Sometimes we fear exposing our flaws, feeling that people will like us less. What we soon learn is that no one is perfect; we all goof up. A true friend understands that and never sports an attitude of superiority or turns our mistakes and weaknesses against us. With them we can dump our insecurities on the doorstep and flop down unfettered, free to be our scratched and blemished selves.

Seen through the eyes of a sincere sidekick, even our little idiosyncrasies take on endearing dynamics. What others criticize as irritating ("Melinda brags nonstop about her kids"), friends transform into virtues ("Melinda's a fabulous mom who always puts her family first"). As author Edna Buchanan puts it, "True friends are those who really know you but love you anyway." At the same time, they should be gently but firmly pushing us toward improvement.

In an article titled "You Gotta Have Friends: How Relationships Keep You Healthy," author Sue Ellin Browder explains how having friends even contributes to our physical health and well-being:

> Scientists don't know exactly how it works, but when we're stressed, depressed, angry, or lonely our brains generate chemical messages that suppress the immune system. Conversely, when we feel happy, hopeful, and loved, the immune system revs up. According to neuroscientist Candace B. Pert, "Our emotions run our immune system."

Here are some ways the article suggests that pals play a part: When we're overwhelmed with external demands, friends provide us a place to pause and get back in touch with what's real. Friends also encourage us to hope, which can be a powerful tool toward healing. Unlike blind optimism, which views the world through rose-colored glasses, "hope sees the dangers and pitfalls along the way but still envisions a path to a better future," explains Harvard Medical School professor Jerome Groopman. Friends instill hope, in part, by valuing us just for ourselves. They let us know we count no matter what, even if we're too tired, old, or ill to be what society calls "productive" or "useful."[1]

The author then describes a friend with a lifelong disease that left her in chronic pain and wheelchair-bound. Yet she somehow retained a ready laugh along with gentle words of comfort and encouragement, something she credits entirely to her faith and her friends. "Just knowing I'm loved and that I matter to others," she is quoted, "strengthens my belief in the ability to keep going."

The article concludes,

> To say that friendship heals is simply to say that love heals. The experts agree: "All open, honest, conscious relationships are spiritual," says Robert F. Lehman, chairman of the Fetzer Institute in Kalamazoo, Michigan, a nonprofit foundation that focuses on the connection between human relationships and health. "They bridge the great divide between our inner and outer lives, and when that happens, there is healing."

Of course, the word "honest" in that quote indicates that there will also be times when, for our ultimate improvement, friends must be brutally blunt with each other. Yet coming from the lips of someone we know truly has our best interest at heart somehow makes the hard truths easier to accept, if not always easy to hear. When truth is traded in love, it inevitably compels us toward being better people. As Proverbs 27:6 reminds us,

"Wounds from a friend can be trusted, but an enemy multiplies kisses."

I wonder. Could that be where the term "kiss-up" came from? Regardless, the scripture makes it clear that to spare ourselves unnecessary stress we should be careful what and in whom we choose to confide. It's been my experience that those who attempt to earn our friendship through overt flattery often harbor a selfish hidden agenda. Consequently, they rarely qualify as people who can be trusted with our most covert confidences.

Undoubtedly there will be times when even our fondest friendships feel a little unevenly matched—where one person seems to be giving more than the other.

The previously mentioned article cites another situation in which the emotionally stronger of two friends sometimes found herself more on the listening than the talking end of their conversations. The interesting twist is that, according to the author, the friend who simply listens could actually be improving his or her own health. To support that statement, she quotes James J. Lynch, a former professor of psychiatry at the University of Maryland Medical School: "When two people get together for a heart-to-heart chat, it's the listener, not the talker, whose blood pressure drops."

Still, in truly healthy relationships, those roles should share at least a semi-equal billing. If not, it's probably a good indication that the friendship is chronically conditional, therefore seriously unstable. The important thing is that the give-and-take stays balanced enough so that neither party feels taken advantage of and tempted to start keeping score. The best way is to practice friendship as the French novelist Alexandre Dumas defined it: "Forgetting what one gives, and remembering what one receives."

This reminds me of a scripture found in Ecclesiates 4:9-12 that reads—

Two are better than one, because they have a good return for their labor: If either of them falls down, one can help the other up. But pity anyone who falls and has no one to help them up. Also, if two lie down together, they will keep warm. But how can one keep warm alone? Though one may be overpowered, two can defend themselves. A cord of three strands is not quickly broken.

Wait a minute—three strands? Where did that extra person come from? Many biblical scholars feel that this suggests including the Lord, that braiding Him into our lives will help us create ropes of relationship that will not soon or easily unravel.

Of course, if a friendship stays one-stranded, that is, one-sided, it is probably time to reconsider whether the reciprocal rewards merit our continued investment of time and emotion. Friendship, to be remedial, must be mutual.

Consider, then, these serious signs of relational avoidance that may indicate people are not capable of carrying on a counterpoised relationship:

- Blatant busyness: they don't mind taking up your time but are always too busy to talk or get together when you want to.
- Tendency to use people: they often ask for favors but are rarely willing to return them.
- Relish the role of the fixer/counselor: they love to come up with solutions for other people's problems but don't take kindly to personal advice or constructive criticism.
- Secretive/fearful of transparency: They thrive on the sordid details of someone else's life but have a hard time venting their own vulnerabilities.

- Competitiveness: They strive to stay several steps above whether materially, intellectually, or physically, needing to feel superior in order to operate from a base of strength.
- Unresolved woundedness: They have been bitterly damaged by life and therefore have no basis of trust on which to build a healthy relationship.

These are people who will, whether consciously or not, inevitably take more out of a relationship than they are capable of giving. With them we'll find ourselves more often stressing than resting. Therefore, it is in our best interest to limit the amount of time and energy we invest in them. As author Irma Kurtz coins it, "Givers have to set limits, because takers rarely do."

The problem is that people don't always fall into clearly labeled categories. We have to find some way of sorting them out. Here's a little exercise excerpted from my book *It All Comes Out in the Wash* that can help. Contributed by my good friend and family counselor Robin Williams Aladeen, I believe it bears repeating.

First, write down everyone we have some sort of ongoing relationship with for, say, the past two years. Circle in green those who are life- and joy-giving, who after spending time with make us feel energized and more alive. These are people we walk away from smiling. Now circle in red those we walk away from feeling tired, depressed, or drained, perhaps even frustrated and angry. If there are those who neither give energy nor take it away, circle them in yellow. These are the "flat-liners," those who have no effect on us either positive or negative.

After doing this, make three columns titled "green," "red," and "yellow," and place the names under the appropriate categories. Sometimes just the graphic realization of how few green people we hang out with and how many red people we do is shocking enough.

The purpose of the exercise is obvious. We all are affected to one degree or another by the people who surround us and who we surround ourselves with. Though we can't completely avoid coming in contact with an agitator every now and then, we need to consciously start saying no to spending a lot of time with people who rub us the wrong way, actively making time for those who soothe and smooth.[2]

What makes it hard is that some of these are colleagues or relatives with whom our paths cross regularly. Additionally, they may have discovered long ago that our codependent doors are always open for them to exchange their stress for solutions or sympathy. How do we break that cycle?

In a recent magazine article titled "The Secret of Beating Fatigue," author Denise Foley suggests that we must first look around our circle of family, friends, and acquaintances to identify what she calls the "seven vampire dwarves—Angry, Whiny, Needy, Grumpy, Nasty, Killjoy, and Toxic."[3]

"On Facebook," she quips, "you can just unfriend them. In real life you have to cope with them." When it comes to contrary colleagues, she suggests using body language to discourage interaction or conversation: turn slightly away, keep working, excuse yourself. Don't ask how they are feeling or what's new.

"If it's a phone conversation, obviously body language won't do. But out-loud language can. 'Oh, I wish I had time to talk!' you can say warmly, without ever explaining why you don't. 'But can you tell me the rest of the story another day?' If it's a family member or close friend, add 'Love you' as you hang up so that hopefully there won't be any hurt feelings."

Avoidance, of course, isn't always the best or most permanent solution. Eventually we have to develop the ability to kindly confront and sweetly but firmly say, "Sorry. I just can't take the time right now." This is especially true in the case of those we have repeatedly tried to help only to discover that they never apply our advice—a sure sign that they are more interested in receiving attention than remedy.

Let me add this important spiritual clarification. In Christian circles we are encouraged and compelled by compassion to interact with all personalities of people. It's called *ministry*. However, there is an appropriate place, method, and timeframe for doing so. The truth is there are some people who need more professional help than we are qualified to give. It is never unspiritual to admit that we are undermining our own mental health by spending an inordinate amount of time trying to solve people's ongoing, sometimes unsolvable problems. In actuality, we may even be hindering them from pursuing professional treatment.

The truth is that we may actually become better spiritual stewards by guarding our time. By reserving more time in our lives for those who positively contribute, we find the emotional balance that better prepares us to cope with the stressful situations when they come.

"Time is the currency of your life," wrote poet and author Carl Sandburg. "It is the only currency you have, and only you can determine how it will be spent. Be careful lest you let other people spend it for you."

Bottom line—we can be good Christians and still understand that not everyone on earth was put here to be our best friend.

That is with perhaps one exception: those known as "man's best friend."

This is as good a place as any to note that some of our most comforting and undemanding companions come in the form of pets. There's just something about the simple but pleasurable interaction between people and animals that can work wonders. Ever notice, for instance, how relaxing it is to repetitively stroke something furry?

Besides that, most pets are extremely affectionate, happy just to have the attention of people they love. They are always glad to see you and never hold a grudge. Having them around easily allows us to transfer the focus from our own problems and put our focus on them. I can't tell you how many times my tears have dampened a dog's fur.

Even if the only menagerie you can manage fits into a fish tank, there's still something mesmerizing and relaxing about watching them swim or scurry. When it comes to rest, we can learn a lot from our pets. They basically eat, sleep, and play or sit staring out the window. Dogs and cats in particular are pros at unplugging and recharging.

If you're looking for a completely unconditional friendship, this is it. The only reciprocal responsibility is found in Proverbs 12:10—"The righteous care for the needs of their animals." So before getting one, consider whether you truly have the time, energy, and patience to care for and enjoy it.

Back to the human form of friendship. Surely if there is any one single foundation, it is summed up in the following quote from well-known nineteenth-century poet and author Ralph Waldo Emerson: "The only way to have a friend is to be one." Again, that means understanding that the kind of companionship covered in this chapter doesn't just automatically happen—it requires time to find and foster.

Here's how the author of the afore-mentioned article, "You Gotta Have Friends," frames it: "To build healthy friendships, you have to make friends a priority. That means you may have to leave the house a bit messier, forego a trip to the mall, or skip watching your favorite sitcom or sports event. But it's a small price to pay for the joys of sharing your life with others."

Seems simple, doesn't it? Yet the true art of making friends in modern society seems to be getting a little sketchy.

As fellow author Cecil Murphy wrote recently, "Everyone wants a friend; not everyone knows how to *be* a friend."

Again, there are some rest-related reasons for that. Sad but true—our crazy-busy culture has caused us all to become a lot more self-absorbed. Looking first to our own needs often leaves little time for sharing our lives with others. Due to overbooked schedules, we routinely run late, sometimes causing us to react rudely to others. Terminally stressed, we stay short-tempered, often allowing our angst to spill over. Neither are qualities that make for really good buddy-building. Nor do we schedule enough "play dates"—times to just sit and enjoy another person's company over coffee or perhaps an afternoon matinee.

Thankfully, though, brotherhood is built not only by hauling the heavy stuff or even by investing huge blocks of time. Certainly standing by those we love during tough times is the true test, yet some of the most reposeful relationships are based as much on the seemingly trivial everyday acts of caring: a silly birthday card, a small but personally meaningful gift, a thoughtful, timely text or e-mail. "The conversations that matter most to people," says University of Iowa professor of communication studies Steve Duck, "are not [always] the long meaning-of-life talks but those that may last only two or three minutes."

Proverbs 25:11-12 poetically puts it this way: "Like apples of gold in settings of silver is a ruling rightly given. Like an earring of gold or an ornament of fine gold is the rebuke of a wise judge to a listening ear." The modern translation *The Message* speaks directly to us jewelry junkies: "The right word at the right time is like a custom-made piece of jewelry, and a wise friend's timely reprimand is like a gold ring slipped on your finger."

There's no doubt that over the years my longtime buddy Marla and I have traded a treasure or two. What truly steers our sistership, though, is to know we can call each other at any time for any reason. The verse on a card I received from her a while back says it all:

> *Call you for coffee,*
> *Call you for prayer*
> *Call you to laugh,*
> *Call you to share.*
> *Thanks, girlfriend, for always being on call!*

Truth is, when you are in the company of someone you've grown comfortable with, words aren't always necessary. Nor do you feel the need to be entertained. As author Eugene Kennedy coins it, "The real test of friendship is: can you literally do nothing with the other person? Can you enjoy those moments of life that are utterly simple?"

Ultimately no one in my life fits that description better than my husband. After forty-five years of marriage, it's not unusual for Jim and me to sit or travel for extended periods of time hardly saying a word. Is it because we've finally run out of things to discuss? No. We still have plenty to talk about. We've simply come to a place of deep companionable contentment in which sometimes just a tender touch or hand squeeze speaks volumes. Truth is, by now we know each other so well that we could probably tell you what the other is thinking at any given moment. Why waste words?

Undoubtedly it takes time to develop the kind of trust in someone that allows us to risk sharing our innermost thoughts and feelings. So what happens when a person we've trusted lets us down? Surely those who have been betrayed in a relationship can be left leery of ever again allowing others to get too close. Yet rather than letting betrayal make us bitter, may I suggest that we try to allow its lessons to help us cultivate wisdom, especially if we recognize a personal pattern of repeatedly choosing friends with the same undependable set of characteristics.

There are a few types of people that Scripture actually instructs us to stay away from. In Proverbs 16:28 Solomon warns us, "A perverse person stirs up conflict, and a gossip separates close friends." Sadly, some even sit in the pews. In Romans 16:17-18 Paul issued this warning to the Early Church: "I urge you, brothers and sisters, to watch out for those who cause divisions and put obstacles in your way that are contrary to the teaching you have learned. Keep away from them. For such people are not serving our Lord Christ, but their own appetites. By smooth talk and flattery they deceive the minds of naive people."

It's obvious that Paul's purpose in issuing this dictum was to protect his true friends and help them embrace healthy relationships. "I want you to be wise about what is good," he states in the next verse, "and innocent about what is evil."

In actuality Paul had plenty of pillow people in his own life whom he describes with great gratitude in the preceding verses of that same chapter. In his other writings as well he often refers to those who have been his close comrades and confidants. Listen to this uncharacteristically sentimental summation found in Philippians 1:7-8, as translated in *The Message:* "You have, after all, stuck with me. . . . All along you have experienced with me the most generous help from God. He knows how much I love and miss you these days. Sometimes I think I feel as strongly about you as Christ does."

This is especially poignant considering that Paul was coming to the end of his earthly ministry. Surely he wanted his friends to know exactly how he felt.

These are the kind of friends we all want, those who will stick with us through every sort of experience. That's why it's important, if we have been previously wounded, to determine not to allow hurtful memories to prevent us from moving on and making new friends. That's not to say making reparation is easy. Unquestionably this will require an act of forgiveness, but it is critical to our continued spiritual and emotional well-being. If wounds are deep or hard to decipher, a trained counselor could be needed to help sort things out.

One important thing to note is that once resolved, we are not obligated to once again embrace these people as best friends, or in the case of abuse, even risk reconciliation. Forgiveness simply frees us to move on and replace those hurtful relationships with healthy ones. As author Doe Zantamata puts it, "Anyone can hold a grudge, but it takes a person with character to forgive. When you forgive, you release yourself from a painful burden. Forgiveness doesn't mean what happened was okay, and it doesn't mean that person should still be welcome in your life. It just means you have made peace with the pain and are ready to let it go."

It might help to recognize that even Jesus, despite being often misunderstood and maligned in His mission, still risked welcoming a few close friends into His life. (See John 15:14-15.) Besides His disciples, the most well-documented were Martha, Mary, and their brother Lazarus, whose door in the city of Bethany was always open to Jesus and His disciples. If you think these were just casual acquaintances, consider John 11:35—the shortest but perhaps most poignant verse in the Bible. After telling of His hearing about the death of Lazarus, it simply states, "Jesus wept."

Seeing the depth of Jesus' feeling for these folks gives us this confidence. Should the time come when we, too, feel as if we've lost our best friend—or perhaps truly have—we can count on the Lord to fill that void. As Proverbs 18:24 puts it, "One who has unreliable friends soon comes to ruin, but there is a friend who sticks closer than a brother." The only one who could be any closer is Christ.

In light of all this, here's a final friendship checklist borrowed from author Gordon MacDonald that we might apply when determining the depth and health of any relationship:

- Who mentors me and offers a baseline of wisdom?
- Who makes me aspire to be a better person?
- Who challenges me to think?
- Who validates my dreams?
- Who cares enough to rebuke me when necessary?
- Who is merciful when I have failed?
- Who shares the load in pressurized moments without being asked?
- Who brings fun and laughter into my life?
- Who gives perspective when I become dispirited?
- Who inspires me to seek faithfully after God?

The bottom line is this: companionship was ordained by God from the very beginning. When He uttered the words in Genesis 2:18, "It is not good for the man to be alone," two things became apparent. God created us for relationship not only with himself but also others. Though He and Adam shared spiritual fellowship, God understood that the only truly suitable earthly helper would be someone with skin on—soft skin.

So let's make it part of our daily "sabbatitude" to seek out as much time as possible with the featherbed friends in our lives—the ones who provide us a place we can sink easily into and enjoy with little effort on either part. At the same time, don't fail to return the favor. As this chapter's key scripture reminds us, whoever refreshes others will be refreshed.

❖ 8 ❖

A PEACEFUL PLACE

*He makes me lie down in green pastures, he leads me
beside quiet waters, he refreshes my soul.*

—Psalm 23:2-3

It was one of those rare-for-midsummer Sacramento Saturdays when the thermometer hit eighty and held. Originating at the ocean, a lovely breeze had blown down the nearby river delta, keeping things comfortable enough for Jim and me to enjoy lunch under the umbrella table on our backyard patio. Afterward—though a long to-do list lurked inside—the lure of the wicker loveseat under our adjacent gazebo won me over. *I'm just going to sit for a minute,* I remember thinking, *and let my lunch settle.* Grabbing a magazine, I didn't make it half-way through before fading into a deliciously sound snooze. What else would one expect in such a peaceful setting?

It was so peaceful, in fact, that my first reflection after waking was not guilt (well, maybe a twinge) but rather how wonderfully refreshed I felt, how unconsciously tired I must have been, and how lovely God looks dressed in nature. It seemed at that same moment the closest to the Garden of Eden I may ever get.

And it should be. My backyard is a place I worked very hard to create when we first moved into our newly-built home twelve years ago. Let me share it with you. Shaded by a perimeter of tall trees and an abundance of flower beds, it contains a curved two-level aggregate patio surrounded by grass. Perched on the higher level is a gazebo complete with overhead fan and padded wicker furniture. Nearby a small rock fountain provides the subtle, soothing sound of trickling water. Three garden boxes file along one fence, behind which deep purple morning glories cascade in delightful disarray. Flower pots and whimsical garden art are tucked in all around. It's an "ahh"-inspiring place specifically designed to celebrate every season.

For twelve successive springs now, I've waited eagerly to welcome the returning turtledoves and robins that deem our gazebo rafters a safe nesting place—something I consider the crowning compliment. During each summer, when the yard is fragrant with herbs, lemon blossoms and jasmine, I've savored the whirring symphony of dragonflies, bees, butterflies, and hummingbirds darting between blooms. As cooler autumn days arrived, I've often sat sweater- or blanket-wrapped, simply letting the leaves and season settle around me. Every winter, as I watch from my window while rain drizzles down outside, the silhouette of the tightly-tucked-in gazebo has seemed to drip with latent promise, bidding me to brighter days ahead.

When weather permits, it also serves as my open-air sanctuary, a place where I can sink in with open Bible or study book, a favorite beverage nearby. It is an atmosphere where thoughts turn easily into prayers, and God seems to whisper back on the breeze.

In case this all seems more aesthetically geared toward the female gender, let me assure you that I have frequently found my husband flopped into one of those pillowed wicker pieces or sitting reflectively at the patio table sipping his early-morning cup of coffee. Though only a few feet away from the family room, it is just far enough to escape ESPN's field of gravity. For the un-indoctrinated, that's the sports channel. As a couple, some of our most significant conversations have been shared there, whether simply recounting the day's events, rehashing some dogged dilemma, or praying fervently for peace or direction.

What a shame it would be to have such a place and not use it. Yet lest you get the impression that we have little other occupation, there are more days than not when all we can do is look longingly in its direction as obligations urge us reluctantly out the door. Thank goodness that when we arrive home, its pacifying presence still waits. Even better are the times when we return from our frequent, too-long times of travel. I like to think of it as the place described in Isaiah 58:11 where "The LORD will guide you always; he will satisfy your needs in a sun-scorched land and will strengthen your frame. You will be like a well-watered garden, like a spring whose waters never fail." We do our best to linger and lap as often as possible.

My hope is that everyone has a similarly refreshing refuge. For as much as we benefit from time spent with friends and family, we each need some special spot where we can slip away alone to pause, sort, and assimilate all the world throws at us. Especially in our age of constant, often unsolicited information—some of it sound, but much confusing and contradictory—it pays to have a place where, as my dad used to say, you can "sit and study for a spell."

Still, these nurturing nooks and comforting crannies do not automatically create themselves. In case you've somehow managed to miss this book's main point, here it is again: we must be intentional about seeking or carving them out, both physically and spiritually. As acclaimed author and fellow solitude seeker Henri Nouwen once wrote, "Discipline is the human effort to create the space in which God can be generous and give you what you need." That, of course, speaks of space in our schedules as well as our environment. Yet I contend that having the latter makes finding the former more likely.

I wonder. *Could King David have been craving such a space as he penned one of the most well-known and soul-soothing passages in Scripture?* "The Lord is my shepherd," begins Psalm 23, "I lack nothing. He makes me lie down in green pastures, he leads me beside quiet waters, he refreshes my soul."

Surely there were countless times when David was more than ready to trade his tumultuous throne for the peaceful pastures of his simpler shepherding days. Instead, since divine calling prevailed, he painted a beautiful word picture of not only that carefree countryside but also the comforting Caretaker who awaits us there, one who guides gently while often urging us to simply lie down and rest a while. Sort of like those calendars with pictures of far-off tropical isles that we stick on our walls to remind ourselves, especially in the wan of winter, that there are warmer and more welcoming places.

Still, the scripture's wording also seems to indicate an age-old dilemma. That is, while the Lord often leads us beside still waters, He may sometimes have a hard time getting us to sit long enough to sip. Why else would it say that he *makes* us lie down in green pastures?

Like sheep, we, too, spend much time with our heads down looking for the proverbial greener pasture, afraid that by taking time out we'll miss something more important. Consequently we often live almost unaware of our surroundings. Nor do we realize how weary our wanderings have made us. Sorry to say, sheep have never been known as the brightest of God's creatures. If the wool fits, friend, wear it.

Neither do we always comprehend how vital our times of solitude are in relationship to everything else we do. This is not merely time stolen from life but necessary to supporting and supplementing it. As my friend Nancie Carmichael wrote in an article based on her wonderful book *Selah: Your Moment to Stop, Think and Step into Your Future,*

> We are not diminished by God-given pauses in life. Instead, we can have greater effectiveness, greater focus. It is to live as Jesus did, periodically getting away from the crush of life to hear from the Father. Then we return, fully involved, fully engaged, fully obedient to God's purpose for us.[1]

Certainly Jesus understood the necessity of finding a place to replenish resources, both physically and emotionally, particularly in the midst of ministry. One scriptural sample is found in Mark 6:31-32: "Then, because so many people were coming and going that they did not even have a chance to eat, he [Jesus] said to them [the disciples], 'Come with me by yourselves to a quiet place and get some rest.' So they went away by themselves in a boat to a solitary place."

Break that down, and we find Christ's fundamental four-part formula: Come with me. Come by yourselves. Come to a quiet place. Get some rest.

Even so, in that instance the boat ride over to the quiet place ended up being the most restful part. The very next verse tells us that unfortunately the crowds followed them. One can only hope that their short sail was pause enough to prepare them for what lay ahead. This included miraculously dividing and delivering lunch for five thousand and Jesus learning that His friend and cousin, John the Baptist, had been beheaded. No small stress. It would not be until after the crowds were fed, both spiritually and physically, that Jesus finally managed to disperse them and make His way up the mountain alone to pray—something else He persistently practiced.

Seeing the benefit in even a short pause, let's refocus for a moment on that word *Selah* used in the title of Nancie's book. To shamelessly plunder her profundity (albeit with permission), let us recognize that it is a biblical word, found mainly in the Old Testament books of Habbakuk and Psalms, inserted at integral places in the text to create a thoughtful pause. According to her research, biblical scholars say the word carries a variety of implications. Some believe it was a musical notation; one Bible translation even uses the word *interlude*. Others say it comes from the Hebrew root word *calah*, meaning to weigh or measure. A few don't even attempt to define it. Based on her own biblical reading, Nancie simply concludes that it serves as a boundary, a marker—"a place," she summates, "to stop and observe, to be still."

She also contends that these *Selahs* are often presented to us in the natural rhythms of life—a day off, Sundays, a vacation, a sleepless night, a time of waiting, or maybe disguised as an interruption. "Then," she writes, "there are the more significant Selahs—the big pauses: A job that's ended. A major loss or illness. Children leaving home. In the crossroads of our journey, we have an opportunity to consider how to proceed meaningfully."

Whether welcome or unwanted, it is important that we train ourselves to take advantage of these stop signs inserted into our lives. These are the times when even a short, well-placed pause can result in remarkable residual benefits, when finding ourselves even momentarily above the fray, we somehow manage to see life from a completely different perspective.

I've made no secret of the fact that flying sometimes freaks me out. And yet there have been many times when, after finally reaching what flight attendants call a "comfortable cruising altitude," I've looked out the airplane window over an ocean of cottony, white clouds and found myself feeling perfectly at peace.

Conversely, it's not surprising that someone who spends much of his or her time in the air might look closer to earth for ease and inspiration. In a recent online interview with Chesley B. "Sully" Sullenberger—the airline pilot now famous for landing his crippled commercial jet in the Hudson River (talk about stress!)—he was asked what ignites his creativity. His answer was "Going for a run. A change of scenery, especially outdoors, literally widens one's perspective and frees the mind."

Point repeated, it pays to have a place where we can slip aside and seek spiritual expansion—some spot that takes us away from the mainstream and puts us in the mind-set of solitude. Especially in the case of significant change or loss, it is essential that we stop and seek a complete change of scenery. When we do, sometimes unexpected things happen.

Even as I began writing this chapter, I was starting a new segment of life. After forty-plus years of sharing our home with family and a few intermittent live-in friends, Jim and I had just recently become full-fledged empty-nesters. Though this was a good and long-awaited change, for me it turned out to be one requiring more adjustment than anticipated. Fact is, I suddenly felt a bit abandoned and a little at loose ends.

Around that same time I had also been scheduled to speak for a women's weekend retreat at South Lake Tahoe, one of northern California's most well-known and breathtakingly beautiful places. It was the perfect environment to seek out a sunny spot between speaking sessions where I could contemplate this new single-family status, pondering as well the wider doors of personal opportunity it offered. Of course, I had also packed along some old ongoing concerns, which, not surprisingly, kept popping out of my mental luggage as well.

Though I knew God had primarily placed me there to speak words of encouragement to that lovely group of ladies, I never imagined how soon I would be receiving some of my own. It was on the last day, as I sat looking out across Lake Tahoe's azure expanse praying specifically for wisdom and direction, that I was unexpectedly approached by a pleasant-looking fellow—someone I presumed was part of another retreat group.

Now before I continue, let me say that to some this next part may seem rather strange. And I suppose it was. Yet, when we truly seek God, especially in the solitude of His own created environment, I believe we should not be surprised by anything He does. Here's what happened.

Without any preliminary introduction whatsoever, the stranger leisurely leaned forward and spoke four simple words: "God's got you covered."

Even as I turned to respond, he spoke again: "The cloud of the Lord is all around you."

Then these final words: "No weapon formed against you will prosper."

That was it—three short sentences. No explanation. No attempt to carry on further conversation. No white robe or halo.

Taken totally off guard, all I could do was stutter rather stupidly, "Th-thank you. That's very . . . affirming."

"You're welcome," he replied with a smile, then turned and walked away. He had delivered his message. He was done.

What in the world could that mean? you must be wondering. Honestly, I had to think about it myself for a few moments. Somehow, though, that "cover concept" felt vaguely familiar. That's when it struck me. How many times in my recent research for this book had I read about God appearing to the Israelites in a cloud by day and a pillar of fire by night—the first for direction, the latter for protection?

Suddenly it made perfect sense. God was assuring me that no matter what difficult decisions lay ahead, He would be there to both lead and linger over me. As for the words about weapons, I would later confirm that they came directly from Scripture—Isaiah 54:17, where God is again speaking to Israel of His future plans to prosper and protect them.

Why He chose such a personal—okay, I'll say it, *angelic*—way to deliver this message, I'll never know. It's far from my usual experience. All I can tell you is that such a feeling of peace fell over me that I had no doubt that both the message and messenger had come from the Lord. At that moment, no part of Lake Tahoe was any deeper than my humble, tearful gratitude.

Surely it was some similar place that inspired songwriter Ralph Carmichael to pen the following:

> *There is a quiet place,*
> *Far from the rapid pace,*
> *Where God can soothe my troubled mind,*
> *Sheltered by tree and flower,*
> *Here in this quiet hour*
> *With Him, my cares I leave behind.*
> *Whether a garden small,*
> *Or on a mountain tall,*
> *New strength and courage there I find,*
> *And from this quiet place,*
> *I go prepared to face,*
> *A new day with love for all mankind.**

What an amazing concept: leaving cares, finding strength and courage, not to mention a new, more loving and optimistic outlook on life! We all need an occasional supernatural shot of inspiration to keep us going.

That's also why, making the most of living in this amazing part of the country, Jim and I plan occasional trips to the near-by Pacific coast. We love walking along the beach, sitting in the sand, just watching the ocean. Those ceaseless waves never fail to remind us of God's continual care.

Certainly we all have our favorite places, and even if they take a little time to reach, they're worth it, especially if we can stay put for a while. My friend Jan has a classic 1940s-era cabin high in the mountains—a place where she has the good fortune to spend much of her summer. She is also a generous person and on several occasions has invited me there for times of re-treat and solitude. What a tremendous treasure to enjoy those lazy, unstructured days with time to write, read, or snooze, perhaps interspersed with a short nature walk. Often we end the day playing board games or watching an old movie. Then it's sleep, awake, and repeat. Occasionally in that relaxed state of mind we've managed to solve some of the world's greatest problems—at least theoretically.

Imagine my amazement, then, to learn that another online author acquaintance, Liz Furman, actually owns an *entire motel*. Located in Dubois, Wyoming, near Yellowstone National Park, she and her family spend the summers there fishing and refur-bishing, undoubtedly in that order. Seems it's also a place that offers times of inspirational solitude as Liz is currently making her first attempt at writing a novel set in that part of 1920s Wyoming. "It's the perfect place to hide out and finish a book project," says Liz, "or just spend some time pondering God's amazing creation. It's one of my favorite places on the planet."

Another way to regain peace and perspective is by revisit-ing places where we've experienced life's happiest moments. My friend Marla just made a pilgrimage to Hume Lake, a southern California retreat center where she spent most summers during her childhood and young adulthood, either as a camper or a counselor. Now seeking some new coordinates on her mid-life map, her hope was that things might clarify themselves when contemplated from the setting where her spiritual journey started. She wasn't disappointed.

In my book *True North: Staying on Course Through Life's Changing Circumstances*, I tell the story of how as young marrieds Jim and I spent one year pastoring a small mission church in an Alaskan fishing village called Pelican. As I was writing that book, we decided to take a trip back in order to sort out a few fuzzy facts. Not only were we able to research but also to reconnect, renewing some old friendships even as we established new ones.

The most important people with whom we reconnected, however, were ourselves—that is, the simpler selves we had been before life's larger responsibilities pressed in upon us. As a result, we've attempted to go back almost every summer since. Not only does Pelican's gorgeous, isolated location make it easy to exit the rat race (just take a left turn at Elfin Cove and keep paddling), but we also somehow still manage to find a few more pieces of our old selves there than anyplace else on earth. And we've been a *lot* of places.

Here's another point to ponder. Even when we can't take a tangible trip back to these poignant places, we can transport ourselves through memories. Surely we've all experienced those "remember when" moments that bring both a smile to the heart and tear to the eye. Now don't get me wrong. I'm not encouraging anyone to live in la-la land. I'm just saying it can be calmingly therapeutic to pay an occasional visit.

Even memories of walking through deep waters can serve to put our hearts at peace. Recalling how the Lord previously pulled us through somehow helps us rest, assured that He will do the same in every future circumstance. Such were the stones of remembrance spoken of in Joshua 4:3. These were twelve rocks—one for each Israelite tribe—taken at God's command from the deepest part of the Jordan River. They were then set up as a memorial of the day God dried up the water so that Israel could cross on dry land.

On her blogspot, "Write Thinking," author Robin Lee Hatcher shares her own reflections on this passage:

And the truth is, we all bring our stones of remembrance from the deepest waters of our lives. Those memorials that I set up by writing . . . or by sharing at a women's retreat, come from deep and oftentimes painful or scary waters. When others see those memorials and ask, "What are these stones?" I can share with them the greatness of God, the places He brought me through, the waters He stopped so I could pass by on dry land.[2]

Another way of clearing our minds and resting our bodies is by enrolling in an exercise program that focuses solely on stretching and relaxation techniques. Research suggests that these activities may even minimize chronic pain, lower blood pressure, sharpen concentration, and with practice, improve the function of the immune system.

There are other relaxation techniques that can be easily incorporated anywhere. Take for instance one I learned years ago that can be done either lying on your back or sitting in a chair. Starting with the forehead, take turns tightening and relaxing individual sets of muscles as you work slowly down your entire body. Doing each set two or three times, you'll be amazed at how rested you feel by the time you get to your toes.

Of course the reality remains that we cannot always conveniently get to our favorite faraway places at the moments we need them most. Nor can we rely solely on good memories or muscle relaxation to help us adequately unwind. This brings us back to carving out places at home—like my gazebo—where the moment we step into them our soul lets out a sigh.

Well-known author Liz Curtis Higgs once shared with a writers group I attended about a separate writing studio she built on her property. "As soon as I walk out the door," she stated, "I literally leave other responsibilities and distractions behind." For some it could be even closer—a favorite sitting room or office, perhaps with a window overlooking a flower bed or fountain. For many guys the current trend toward a "man cave" might be just the (game) ticket. Marla has a place she calls her prayer corner. It is little more than a comfortable chair situated between a window and the French doors leading to her patio. On one side is a small table, on the other a basket holding her Bible and other inspirational reading material. Yet it is a sweet spot reserved only for the times when she turns her attention to the Lord.

Truth is, every room in our home and workplace can exude an atmosphere of serenity. Sometimes it's as simple as choosing a soothing or cheerful paint color. Add to that a few strategically placed items that remind or encourage us to unwind. Perhaps photos of a favorite family vacation or some small plaques such as the ones I have in my office and family room that say "Relax" or "Keep It Simple." Another that graces our master bedroom even helps remind Jim and me how little it takes to put a peck of restful romance back in our marriage. It simply says: "Always Kiss Me Goodnight."

There's something, too, about the serene sense of order that comes through repetitive routine. Even if it's nothing more than the every-morning act of brewing that first pot of coffee and then—as my husband (bless him!) always does—carrying a cup to someone we love. And don't forget the calming effect that comes from mindless tasks like making the bed, puttering around the garage, or folding laundry.

Speaking of laundry, how about the joy of jumping into those soft, often-washed sweats, tee-shirts, or slippers? Clean sheets, too, can feel so soothing. Years ago I established the habit of always changing the bed before we leave on a trip. That way, whatever time we wearily arrive home, we can quickly shower and slide right in. Likewise, I can hardly wait to slip right back into my regular schedule. These are such small things, but the soul-soothing pleasure they add to our daily lives is amazing.

Then there is the sense of security we find in knowing there are things we can count on, things that will never, or rarely ever, change. Surely that explains why we feel such solitude when stepping outside on those clear, moonless nights and looking up at the vast array of stars, or on a night when the moon is full and turns the landscape luminescent. Nothing on earth is more dependable than the stars and seasons. Scripture backs my belief that God set them into being just to give us a sense of stability and continuity.

I don't think it would be a stretch to imagine that between Egypt and Canaan, Moses spent more than a few sleepless nights during which he stepped outside his tent and turned his eyes toward heaven. This may have been what inspired him to write the soul-stabilizing words found in Psalm 90:1-2, "Lord, you have been our dwelling place throughout all generations. Before the mountains were born or you brought forth the whole world, from everlasting to everlasting you are God." Surely in that vast starry array He, too, found a source of strength and security, as well as the assuring reminder that the God who flung them into the sky was well able to perform all He had promised.

Come to think of it, that's not a bad thing for us to consider either, in light of how unstable our world has become. Truth is, sometimes the most peaceful place we can imagine *is* in heaven. It is there, Scripture says, that Jesus is also carving out a place—not for himself but for us. Hear in John 14:1-3 Christ's own comforting words: "Do not let your hearts be troubled. You believe in God; believe also in me. My Father's house has many rooms; if that were not so, would I have told you that I am going there to prepare a place for you? And if I go and prepare a place for you, I will come back and take you to be with me that you also may be where I am."

Contrary to popular political belief, the world will never negotiate permanent peace. Yet in the midst of colliding current events, our hearts, souls, and minds can still find spiritual refuge in that blessed hope.

In the meantime, there will undoubtedly be those moments when we want nothing more than to simply hide from all that swirls around us. How well I remember as a small child discovering a spot between some large bushes surrounding my grandmother's house where, after I crawled in, the branches would close around me. Once inside, no one could see me. It was my secret spot, carved out and covered over.

Maybe that's why one of my very favorite Bible passages is Psalms 91:3-4—"Surely he [the Lord] will save you from the fowler's snare and from the deadly pestilence. He will cover you with his feathers, and under his wings you will find refuge; his faithfulness will be your shield and rampart."

No matter what happens, to repeat the words of the Lake Tahoe stranger, God has us covered. So this chapter's steps toward "sabbatitude" are these: Let's learn to take advantage of every pause life presents us. At the same time, make an effort to carve out at least one special place where we can conveniently slip away and be still before the Lord. For it is not in the places alone that we find peace but in His presence.

❖ 9 ❖
RESTING ON HIS PROMISES

You will keep in perfect peace those whose minds
are steadfast, because they trust in you.
—Isaiah 26:3

On a countertop near my fridge sits a small, sapphire-blue plastic box. Its corners are cracked with age, its hinges broken. It is molded to resemble a small treasure chest, and truly it is. For tucked inside are at least one hundred fifty narrow, yellow-edged cards on which specially selected Bible verses have been printed. Embossed on top of the box in faded gold letters are two simple words: "Precious Promises." More than mere snippets of instant inspiration, these represent a sample of the spiritual truths on which our family has long relied.

The first time I remember seeing that box was on my Grandma Witt's kitchen table, which means it has to be over fifty years old. Every time we visited, it was her custom that before our meals we each picked a card and read it. Yet Grandma's original appropriation of these promises goes much farther back than that. She was, in fact, the first person on my father's side of the family to "get religion," committing her life to Christ at an old-fashioned revival meeting sometime in the early 1920s.

According to my parents, this auspicious event made an almost instantaneous and drastic difference in not only the way Grandma lived her life but also how she determined her children and grandchildren would live theirs. From that moment on, she began a personal campaign to put those promises into play, impressing them onto her family's hearts and minds. That—along with a heaping helping of newfound holiness—resulted in all six of her children eventually coming to receive God's greatest gift and promise of eternal life through faith in His Son, Jesus Christ.

After Grandma passed away, the blue box came to rest on a prominent bookshelf in my parents' home. At some point it was passed along to me. Its current place on my counter serves as a daily reminder of the faith that so many of my predecessors have, over the years, put in those promises. Often, especially on life's most difficult days, I have reflected on those before me who have pulled out a card or two, finding in those words the most precious promise of all: God's peace, which Philippians 4:7 says "transcends all understanding."

Of course, putting God's promises into perpetuation requires a bit more effort than just snatching out an occasional scrap of scripture or viewing them—as some might—like fortune cookie fillers. In order to accurately appropriate them, we have to study a bit before understanding all that's available to us. Though you can still buy those little promise boxes if you wish, they contain only a few of the more than three thousand scattered throughout the entire Bible. Therefore, the best way of becoming familiar is to ferret them out for ourselves, which means reading our Bibles regularly. As we discipline ourselves to do so, it has been my experience that God will illuminate an appropriate assurance for every situation. What may help us be more diligent is to see that time itself as a small Sabbath.

At the same time, there's no religious rule against seeking out the scriptures that specifically address our most current area of need. This is where the alphabetized concordance at the back of many Bibles comes in handy, helping us quickly track down a topic. Consider these practical personalizing suggestions taken from a set of online sermon notes by Pastor Ken Brandon:

> In general, choose a particular list of verses that apply to a specific present need and start reading them through. Ask the Lord to make them come "alive" to you by the power of the Holy Spirit. Turn those verses . . . into prayers of faith, praise, and thanks. Pray them frequently to the Lord [and] soon they will be memorized in the heart [becoming] the channel for the power of God to work.[1]

Pastor Ken also suggests that as we read the Word daily, we start our own lists under different headings. In this way we will not only be building future Scripture references, but we will also have easier access to promises we might want to share with others. Citing personal practice, he states, "These lists of scriptures have been accumulated over the years and recorded in the blank pages at the back of my Bible"—yet another good suggestion.

Looks like Grandma knew that, too, since something else I inherited was a couple of her well-worn Bibles. As I leafed through those dog-eared, much-marked pages, two things became apparent. She was not only a devoted student of the Word—she was also a person well acquainted with the world's tests and trials. How could I tell? As was common in her day, pressed between her Bible's pages are some mementos of the lives and times that touched hers.

The ones I found most intriguing include a lock of white hair belonging to my grandfather, who had passed away unexpectedly on a long-ago Christmas Eve; a few four-leaf clovers, flower petals, and leaves (special because perhaps they were picked and proudly presented by a child or grandchild); a newspaper clipping detailing the mysterious death of 1930s evangelist Aimee Semple McPherson—someone my grandmother had mightily admired only to discover along with the rest of the world that, common to all humanity, she had feet of clay; and a faded photo accompanied by a yellowed, now almost illegible letter from her youngest son, written while he was stationed in Korea during the 1950s military conflict.

More than mere memorabilia, to me these represent some of life's most basic human emotions—grief, joy, disappointment, and fear; those that most commonly cause us to turn toward God and His word for comfort, guidance, and reassurance. Obviously it's something my grandmother did often. But the fact that rather than just sacredly putting her Bible back on the shelf, she made it a scrapbook of her spiritual journey, reveals it as even more intimate.

In specific reference to the precious promises found in God's Word, perhaps no passage of Scripture captures God's overall guarantee—and Grandma's spiritual grit—any better than 2 Peter 1:3-4: "His [Christ's] divine power has given us everything we need for a godly life godliness through our knowledge of him who called us by his own glory and goodness. Through these he has given us his very great and precious promises, so that through them you may participate in the divine nature, having escaped the corruption of the world caused by evil desires."

According to our previously quoted online pastor, there are a few points taken from this passage worth elaborating. First, a promise doesn't mean much unless it's personally directed. This scripture confirms that God's promises are directly pointed at *us* as born-again believers. Second, these aren't just ordinary, everyday promises—the kind we humans are prone to make glibly with no undergirding guarantee. They are, to use the King James wording, "exceeding great and precious," meaning beyond natural limits (supernatural), surpassing all others, and of such value that a suitable price is hard to estimate. Claiming them gives us the impetus not only to turn from the world's way of thinking but also to become active participants in God's great eternal plan.

As it relates to resting in them, consider with me for a moment the dictionary definition of a promise. Abbreviating Webster's wording, it is "an oral agreement to do or not do something . . . to give a basis for expectation."

I don't know about you, but I've made a lot of "oral agreements"—both to God and others, giving a "basis for expectation," which at that moment I fully intended to keep but to my great shame sometimes failed to follow through. There were also times when, despite my dogged determination, I was simply unable fulfill my oral agreement, usually because I hadn't accurately assessed the situation or fully understood the impact of my obligation.

That's what makes God's promises different. We can unfailingly depend on both His faithfulness and His ability to fulfill them. "Let us hold unswervingly to the hope we profess," Hebrews 10:23 encourages us, "for he who promised is faithful." How do we know? Starting from Creation, every story recorded in the Bible shows us how God came through for His children. Why wouldn't we believe that He will continue doing so?

As for ability, surely He who first flung the stars into the sky and spoke the world into being has the power to perform all He has promised the more problem-prone part of His creation. Here's how Jeremiah 32:17 juxtaposes it against nature: "Ah, Sovereign LORD, you have made the heavens and the earth by your great power and outstretched arm. Nothing is too hard you.'"

The more we read the Bible the more familiar we become with its Author, which means we come to better understand His loving, faithful, and unchanging nature, along with His limitless power. If at times He comes across as harsh and judgmental, it is always because of people who failed to trust Him and took matters in their own hands. Whatever questions we might conjure or encounter are all answered in His word. As Proverbs 30:5 assures us, "Every word of God is flawless; he is a shield to those who take refuge in him."

Put Him to the test, and what we will find is that not only can we trust God to make good on every promise given, but we can also take rest and refuge in it. For me, no promise passage in Scripture sums this up any better than Psalm 91:1-2: "Whoever dwells in the shelter of the Most High will rest in the shadow of the Almighty. I will say of the LORD, 'He is my refuge and my fortress, my God, in whom I trust.'"

Judging from that, here's another interesting thought. It would seem that rest equals trust as much as trust equals rest. To come to the place in which we truly rest in God's promises means we stop striving to work things out ourselves. Yet it is so easy to fall into the trap of feeling that if we are not physically doing something, we are not concerned or proactive. Problem is, our striving usually produces exhaustion, which only exacerbates our problems, even causing us to make more poor decisions and create continued chaos. Somehow we must retrain ourselves to see trust as active, not passive. The same goes for prayer, which is trust's necessary counterpart.

If we strive for anything, let it be as Paul instructed in 1 Timothy 4:9-10: "This is a trustworthy saying that deserves full acceptance. That is why we labor and strive, because we have put our hope in the living God, who is the Savior of all the people, and especially of those who believe."

Truth is, trusting and waiting may sometimes be the hardest work we do. Listen to how eloquently my friend Nancie Carmichael expressed this in a recent online post:

> Oh . . . how hard it is for me to wait! Today Psalm 37:7 speaks to me: "Rest in the LORD, and wait patiently for him." Too often waiting doesn't feel productive; it feels like wasted time. And yet if I stop—be still and notice—that's when real progress is made. What—or who—is right in front of me? How do I respond now? We can miss the beauty and opportunity that is right before us by being consumed with the next assignment, the next challenge.
>
> Waiting on God takes practice, active listening. It's an inner listening, even in the midst of activity. Waiting does not mean to be in control but to cultivate the place to respond to the Holy Spirit's leading. So we plan. And we wait. Then respond. "Lord, you said if we wait on you, you will renew our strength. Thank you for reminding me to wait on you for your timing, your way, your purpose."

Nancie's prayer emphasizes another good point. While many of God's promises can be appropriated immediately—particularly those involving salvation, sanctification, protection, and direction—there are some in His own sovereign oversight that we have to wait for. This means we must also trust His timing.

Admittedly, this can become hard, especially when we claim a promise but don't see any immediate results, or when our prayers are not answered in the way we hoped they would. Yet 2 Peter 3:9 assures us—"The Lord is not slow in keeping his promise, as some understand slowness. Instead he is patient with you, not wanting anyone to perish, but everyone to come to repentance."

Wait a minute. Patient with *us*? Aren't *we* the ones being patient here—waiting for God to make good on His promise?

Yes, but here's where the not-so-small matter of accepting God's sovereignty comes in. When He doesn't act immediately, we must understand that it's because He has an eternally bigger and better plan—one often involving the welfare of others as well. How selfish we are to forget that we are not the only people who are praying or about whom God is concerned! Even more important are the lessons learned and spiritual growth experienced in the process.

The bottom line is this: God has a much larger—as in *universal*—perspective than we do. As Isaiah 55:8-9 reminds us: "'My thoughts are not your thoughts, neither are your ways my ways,' declares the LORD. 'As the heavens are higher than the earth, so are my ways higher than your ways and my thoughts than your thoughts.'"

Verses 10 and 11 then help us see how the end result is not only for His higher purpose but also for our ultimate good: "As the rain and the snow come down from heaven, and do not return to it without watering the earth and making it bud and flourish, so that it yields seed for the sower and bread for the eater, so is my word that goes out from my mouth: It will not return to me empty, but will accomplish what I desire and achieve the purpose for which I sent it."

Perhaps our greater issue is not the matter of *putting* our problems in His hands but *leaving* them there. This means backing away and allowing Him to work, which—let's be honest— usually happens only once we recognize that we are powerless to do anything about the situation ourselves.

A great illustration of this came to me in a story from my friend Loretta Steiger. It seems that earlier this year she arrived at her Colorado Springs home to discover a doe and brand-new fawn hovering over one of her basement window wells. The frantic bleating coming from inside led Loretta to discover that a twin fawn had fallen in and could not get out. Being a woman of both compassion and action, she quickly grabbed some work gloves and walked slowly toward the mother deer, all the while talking as gently as possible.

"I feared she would attack me as I came close to her baby," admits Loretta, "but to my amazement she backed off and calmly watched as I lifted the fawn out and set it on the ground." The family of three then trotted down the hill as Loretta breathed a sigh of relief.

"I know I cannot assume that the doe had any sense of reasoning," Loretta concluded, "but it seemed to me that a measure of trust came over her and she allowed me to fix the problem. What a simple but profound lesson for us: to trust God means we must back away and let Him fix things."

Loretta admits that the incident caused her to reflect somewhat regretfully on the times throughout her life when she did not rise to such a level of trust and, attempting to bring difficult trials to an end, took things into her own hands. Now she can see how her life lessons have brought her to a more simple and uncomplicated place of faith.

On top of that, she had also recently read through Psalm 37. "Its overall message stating 'don't fret, trust God' has become a new revelation to me on a daily basis," she added. "The more I trust, the more I relax and enjoy God."

Loretta has hit on another important point. Trust is not something we employ once and forever. Like everything "pertaining to life and godliness," it must be renewed on a daily—sometimes hourly—basis. No wonder when the Israelites cried out for food, the manna God gave them was only good for one day or, in the case of the Sabbath, two (see Exodus 16:14-36).

Besides simply sending food, He was teaching them the principle of trusting Him daily for provision even as they anticipated their ultimate arrival in the Promised Land.

Surely no one in Scripture received any greater number of promises from God than the Israelites. Time and again He told them either directly or indirectly what He intended to do on their behalf. Basically this boiled down to freeing them from slavery and leading them to a permanent resting place, all the while directing and protecting. Wouldn't you say that pretty much sums it up for us as well?

Yet, as we've already seen, they were an impatient, anxious, and overeager lot, often doubtful and consequently disobedient. Despite all God's miracles, despite His obvious ongoing presence, the desert's dust clouded their vision, making it hard for the Israelites to keep their eyes focused on His place of promise.

If this resonates with anyone, take heed. As a result, the Israelites' wanderings extended for forty years. That could also happen to us if, rather than resting in God's promises, we continue to insist on taking things into our own hands. One can only wonder how much anxiety and ultimate grief they might have saved themselves if they had only held firm to God's original guarantee.

The good news is that despite their disbelief, God kept His promises to Israel. Joshua 21:43-45 tells us—

So the LORD gave Israel all the land he had sworn to give their ancestors, and they took possession of it and settled there. The LORD gave them rest on every side, just as he had sworn to their ancestors. Not one of their enemies withstood them; the LORD gave all their enemies into their hands. Not one of all the LORD's good promises to Israel failed; every one was fulfilled.

God's promises are amazing. Even on the days when we have trouble trusting, it doesn't change them. God stands by His Word. He will never go back on what He has promised to do. "If we are faithless," states 2 Timothy 2:13, "he remains faithful, for He cannot disown himself."

Let's be honest. As humans, we find that there's unbelief in all of us. That's why we can also identify with the story in Mark 9:17-24 of a man who in desperation brought his demon-possessed son to Jesus for healing. After describing the boy's problem, the father said to Jesus, "If you can do anything, take pity on us and help us."

"'If you can'?" said Jesus. "Everything is possible for one who believes."

"I do believe!" the boy's father exclaimed, then recognizing his verbal slip, quickly added, "Help me overcome my unbelief!"

Like the man in the story, we must recognize this readiness in ourselves and ask God to help us hold on without wavering. Still it's no secret that the enemy knows how to work on our weakness. Ever notice, for instance, how much easier it is for us to remain optimistic during daylight hours? No wonder the enemy often comes under cover of darkness, bringing doubt and growing normal concerns to gigantic proportions. That's when it pays to repeat Hebrews 11:1—"Now faith is confidence in what we hope for and assurance about what we do not see"— or as V. Raymond Edman put it, "Never doubt in the dark what God told you in the light."

The best way to keep our minds from traveling the devil's dark, desolate roads is to throw up a biblical roadblock. Using Jesus' example when He was tested in the wilderness (Matthew 4:1-11,) we must pummel him with God's promises. In that way, we are not only reminding him of what God has guaranteed, but we're reassuring ourselves as well.

Here's another suggestion. Pray God's promises instead of the problem. Since His Word never comes back void, these prayers are surely a shoo-in. "This is the confidence we have in approaching God," 1 John 5:14 tells us, "that if we ask anything according to his will, he hears us."

Or try expressing trust by praising God not only for what He's already done but also for what He has promised to do. Undoubtedly this sometimes requires what Hebrews 13:15 calls a "sacrifice of praise"—again thanking Him for what we know even if we don't presently see or feel it. Yet Psalm 22:3 indicates that because He is "enthroned" in our praise, meaning He inhabits it, the enemy can't keep that kind of company and won't hang around.

Of course we can't always sit back and wait for God to do everything. Some promises depend on our participation. James 2:17 tells us, "In the same way, faith by itself, if it is not accompanied by action, is dead." Just make sure before plunging in that it is prayer-led participation.

I would also be remiss if I didn't mention that while some promises are effective only to believers who appropriate them, others are true regardless of whether we believe them or not. Take for instance Paul's partial proclamation in Romans 8:13— "If you live according to the flesh, you will die;" or when he reminds us in 1 Timothy 6:7 that "We brought nothing into the world, and we can take nothing out of it"—tough words but true.

Surely three of the hardest areas to trust God with are relationships, finances, and health. I mentioned earlier that all of my Grandma Witt's children eventually came to receive salvation in the Lord. Sadly, not all of them stuck with it. Why? Suffice it to say that the gift of free will Adam and Eve opened in the garden allows more decision-making leeway than some can wisely handle. This is something we've also experienced with our own children. My first book, *Prodigal in the Parsonage: Encouragement for Ministry Leaders Whose Child Rejects Faith*, chronicles the story of our long and difficult journey, particularly with our oldest son.

Still, like Grandma, we have never given up believing that one day our children will all be wholeheartedly serving God. The personal assurance I have claimed is 2 Timothy 1:12: "I know whom I have believed, and am convinced that he is able to guard what I have entrusted to him until that day." It is one with which, especially on the days when it's tempting to throw in the towel, I have repeatedly encouraged myself. Whatever our assortment of broken or battered relationships, God's Word has equally as many applicable assurances we can claim.

As for finances, perhaps a promise found in Philippians 4:19 will offer hope: "My God will meet all your needs according to the riches of his glory in Christ Jesus." Let's not forget that God is not only our Creator but also our great Provider. Whatever we truly need in the area of resources, financial or otherwise, God can supply. At the same time He can give us the wisdom and discipline to devise and implement our own plan for downsizing debt.

Health issues are another hard thing. Though we have God's promise of healing, we've all known those who, despite a plethora of prayers, have not been bodily restored. The reality is that God sometimes chooses to heal us here on earth; other times He performs the ultimate healing by taking us to heaven. In the midst of His own life-and-death struggle, in Psalm 31:14-15 David expressed his faith in both God's ability and sovereignty: "I trust in you, Lord; I say, 'You are my God.' My times are in your hands."

There's no denying it. Bad things happen to good people. This is undoubtedly where trust plays the biggest part. When things come along that we simply can't control, we must ask

God to give us wisdom and direction to determine the best course of both treatment and action. The ultimate outcome, however, must be left with the Lord.

The good news is that whatever path God chooses for us, He promises to walk it with us. "Never will I leave you; never will I forsake you," Hebrews 13:5 assures us. This is actually a quote from Joshua 1:5, where the Lord tells Joshua, "No one will be able to stand against you all the days of your life. As I was with Moses, so I will be with you; I will never leave you nor forsake you." Undoubtedly this was a card Joshua pulled out of his promise box often. It was the same promise that Jesus gave His disciples in Matthew 28:20—"Surely I am with you always, to the very end of the age," or as the King James Version puts it, "even unto the end of the world."

As my friend Marla likes to say, "You always know it's God when He repeats himself." Still it is reassuring to know, especially in the case of a heaven-bound healing, that His repeated promise includes walking us all the way home.

One of my most inspiring recent examples of trusting God in such a circumstance came earlier this year when one of our dearest long-time friends and ministry colleagues unexpectedly died. Glen Cole had been not only a long-time pastor and denominational leader but also someone held in high esteem throughout the entire Sacramento community. The prior picture of health, his sudden death from heart failure came as a shock to many, but none more than his wife, Mary Ann.

Yet the very next Sunday she was in church, determined to address and allay the concerns of their grieving congregation. Surrounded on the platform by family, she offered a brief but eloquent explanation of the week's earlier events and then offered a few words assuring everyone that she was doing fine. It was her last words, however, that we'll all best remember: "What else can I tell you," she stated, "except that I trust my God?"

Surely many marveled at the spiritual strength of this petite, elegant lady. Yet through fifty-eight years of marriage and ministry, this had been her and Glen's godly way of life. Why would it be any different now? To me, her example epitomizes our chapter's theme scripture from Isaiah 26:3: "You will keep in perfect peace those whose minds are steadfast, because they trust in you."

The key word here is "steadfast," which Webster's dictionary defines as: (1) fixed or unchanging; steady (2) firmly loyal or constant; unswerving. Like my friend MaryAnn, we must condition ourselves not to consider any other option. Sometimes that means re-reading and repeating to ourselves what we know is true even when everything else seems to contradict it. Whatever the circumstances around us, however hopeless things look, we must continue to believe that more is happening in the heavenly realm than we can possibly know or see.

This steadfast mind-set was something the apostle Paul attempted to communicate to the Early Church when he wrote in 2 Corinthians 1:18-20, "As surely as God is faithful, our message to you is not 'Yes' and 'No.' For the Son of God, Jesus Christ, who was preached among you by us—by me and Silas and Timothy—was not 'Yes' and 'No,' but in him it has always been 'Yes.' For no matter how many promises God has made, they are 'Yes' in Christ. And so through him the 'Amen' is spoken by us to the glory of God."

In other words, if we know that God through Christ has given us His glorious "Yes," we must persistently practice putting our own hearty "Amen!" of agreement on it. Let me be quick to restate that this doesn't mean God never says no. But rest assured—when He does, it's because He has a bigger yes planned for the future.

For me nothing epitomizes all of the above better than a well-known hymn I learned in childhood, one I've sung often to myself through many troubled times:

> 'Tis so sweet to trust in Jesus,
> Just to take Him at His Word,
> Just to rest upon his promise;
> Just to know: "Thus saith the Lord."
> O how sweet to trust in Jesus,
> Just to trust His cleansing blood,
> Just in simple faith to plunge me
> 'Neath the healing, cleansing flood!
> Yes, 'tis sweet to trust in Jesus,
> Just from sin and self to cease,
> Just from Jesus simply taking
> Life and rest, and joy and peace.
> I'm so glad I learned to trust Thee,
> Precious Jesus, Savior, Friend;
> And I know that Thou art with me,
> Wilt be with me to the end.
> Jesus, Jesus, how I trust Him!
> How I've proved Him o'er and o'er!
> Jesus, Jesus, precious Jesus!
> O for grace to trust Him more!
> —Louisa M. R. Stead

This brings us, then, to the basic truth of the gospel. While humanity seeks solace by many different ways and means, it is only when putting our trust in Christ and God's continuing covenants that we find a place of spiritual resolution resulting in rest. We must conclude as Simon Peter did in John 6:68, "Lord, to whom shall we go? You have the words of eternal life. We have come to believe and to know that you are the Holy One of God."

Like Grandma and a host of glory-bound graduates before us, the foremost promise we must claim is that of salvation as outlined in 1 John 1:9: "If we confess our sins, he [God] is faithful and just and will forgive us our sins and purify us from all unrighteousness."

From that point on, everything else we accomplish in our Christian life is based on grasping God's great store of guarantees, then learning to rest in reliance on them. Most amazing of all is that as we develop a steadfast "sabbatitude" of trust in the small things, the easier it becomes to lean on Him through life's largest challenges.

❖ 10 ❖
SWAPPING YOUR SPECS

Do not conform to the pattern of this world,
but be transformed by the renewing of your mind.
—Romans 12:2

Autumn is my favorite season. Yet here in northern California summer temperatures often linger late into the year. This means that other than in the high country, it's usually early November before things cool off enough for the season's correlating colors to emerge. For a former Midwestern gal, this is frustrating. Last year, however, I accidentally found a remedy. I bought a pair of brown-tinted sunglasses, which, unnoticed at the time of purchase, cause things to take on a golden hue. Now to get my "fall fix" all I have to do is put on my autumn-colored glasses. Unlike their proverbial rose-colored counterpart, I still see the world clearly—but a whole lot more warmly.

Likewise, if we are ever to truly change our harried, hurried habits, we're going to have to swap our spiritual specs, replacing them with ones that will help us neutralize negative thinking and produce a more positive, peaceful life perspective. "Change your thoughts," said popular 1960s pastor, author, and positive-thinking proponent Norman Vincent Peale, "and you change your world."

Obviously this requires more than just bobbing in a harbor of happy thoughts surrounded by a fog of fairy dust. According to a more current positive-but-practical author, Gordon Mac-Donald, it means "we must be reforming and reframing regularly by taking time to inquire of the soul, reflect on our relationships, and reframe all the pieces of life into what God originally wanted us to be."

Sounds a little like work, doesn't it?

Still, so much stress and unrest incubates in our mind where flawed facts, even fabrication, rob us of peace and harmony with God and others. Like a poorly tuned piano, an anxious, negative outlook can cause us to live off-key, even discordant—anything but restful or enjoyable. Surely a warmer outlook is worth setting our sights on.

This means we must not be sidetracked by those who feel it is merely human nature to focus on negativity, as if there were nothing we can do to counteract it. In one article Martin Seligman, author of *Flourish: A Visionary New Understanding of Happiness and Well-being,* admits, "The mind is like your tongue, swishing around life, looking for a cavity."[1] The article attributes this to a theory that throughout history the humans who survive are those who see trouble coming. There is no mention of the maladies that sometimes blindside us.

Whether due to nature or nurture, it's obvious to me that there's only one way we're going to change what my friend Jan calls "stinkin' thinkin'." That is, as this chapter's key scripture, Romans 12:2, indicates, by transforming our worrisome, worldly outlook into a hopeful, heavenly one. Obviously this requires lifting our eyes and hearts a little higher.

When it comes to pessimism, psychological experts agree that while negative thinking is nothing new, it requires regular rectifying. As one online inspirational writer put it, "Enlightenment is not about knowing as much as it is about *unknowing*; it is not so much learning as *unlearning*."[2]

Attitude adjustment was something the apostle Paul often addressed when writing to the Early Church. Fortunately for us all, in Philippians 4:4-9 he provided a fail-proof formula, one that I believe with a little mental maneuvering can be consistently incorporated. Let's see what he suggests.

"Rejoice in the Lord always" Paul begins in verse 4. "I will say it again: Rejoice!" Though Paul uses repetition to reinforce his main point, to me the key words here are actually *in the Lord* and *always*. After all, anyone can whoop it up when things are going well, but what of the times when circumstances swirl chaotically about us? It's then we must dig deep to discover what—or Who—we really have to rejoice about.

Perhaps nothing illustrates this better than hearing stories from survivors of recent disasters such as Hurricane Sandy, some of whom lost all their earthly possessions or were forced to live for weeks without water, heat, or electricity. Yet what we witness time and again is how people's real inner spirits inevitably emerge. Granted, many were initially grateful just to be alive. But at the same time, with relatively few exceptions, the highest in human nature soon seemed to surface. Within hours of the storm's passing, neighbors and disaster relief agencies were reaching out, offering help, hope, and encouragement.

One of the sweetest stories I heard was about a stack of World War II love letters that were found washed up on the beach. The family who discovered them determined to track down the couple who had written them, only to learn that the husband had already passed away and the now-ninety-one-year-old wife was in poor health. Still, it's a great illustration of how love survives the storms of life, both symbolically and literally.

It's sad to think that it takes a hurricane to help us sort out what's really important. But it's times like those—which, by the way, seem to be occurring more frequently—when we are all reminded that when everything else is swept away, it's *only* in the Lord that we have hope and are able to truly rejoice, not necessarily in our circumstances but despite them. As Psalm 62:1-2 reminds us, "Truly my soul finds rest in God; my salvation comes from him. Truly he is my rock and my salvation; he is my fortress, I will never be shaken."

While none of us would wish disaster on anyone, the fact is that without a few tough times, we all tend to take a lot for granted. Undoubtedly that's why one article titled "Got Gratitude?" encourages us to occasionally recall them. "Make a list of bad breaks you've faced," it states. "Recounting what you've been through—and survived—will help you appreciate what you have now. Ask yourself: What personal strengths grew out of the experience? How has it helped me value the important things? This provides new perspective on life's hardships."[3] In the words of yet another golden church oldie, by Johnson Oatman Jr., *Count your blessings; name them one by one. Count your many blessings; see what God has done.*

"Let your gentleness be evident to all," is Paul's next admonition in Philippians 4:5. "The Lord is near." It doesn't take disaster to discover that we live in an increasingly angry, jump-to-judgment world, not to mention an age of entitlement. As addressed in an earlier chapter, all we have to do is drive a busy freeway, listen as we stand in a slow-moving line, or turn on the television set. Society everywhere is seething and looking for someplace to stick the blame. If there were ever a time when cool heads and gentle spirits need to prevail, it is today. In most cases this means guarding not only our minds but also our mouths. As Proverbs 15:1 reminds us, "A gentle answer turns away wrath, but a harsh word stirs up anger."

Sorry to say, some of us can even get a bit overzealous when trying to make a good point. Though there's nothing wrong with sharing honest opinions, we shouldn't become infuriated with others for not always agreeing. The same is true of sharing our Christian faith. While it is an important and mandated part of being a believer, little good is accomplished when we allow our evangelistic efforts to escalate into a heated argument. In most cases this not only pushes people away, but it also trashes our testimony. Again, according to Paul, the best and most convincing endorsement for our faith and strong feelings is when they are guided by a gentle spirit.

Certainly there will be times in life when we can't help getting a little ticked off, but if anger becomes a persistent, alienating issue, it might help to consider this practical suggestion from the above-referenced article: "Know your hot-button issues. Everyone possesses a few deeply held beliefs that lead to overreaction in response to daily incidents. Do you experience extreme emotions about things that should be no big deal? You may want to delve into your history to see what's simmering underneath the surface. If your personal life is complicated or difficult, enlist help—either from good friends or a therapist."

My life observation has been that the things we worry, grieve, or harbor anger over serve no positive purpose. On the contrary, they wear us out, stealing our joy and sapping our spiritual strength. As Old Testament governor Nehemiah reminded the remorseful, law-lamenting Israelites, "Do not grieve, for the joy of the Lord is your strength" (Nehemiah 8:10).

Again, it's a matter of putting things into spiritual perspective, which is where the second part of Philippians 4:5 comes into play: "The Lord is near." Whether we interpret Paul's reminder as referring to Christ's promised second coming or God's everyday omnipresence, it should motivate us to react in ways that will be pleasing to Him and uplifting to others.

In actuality both scenarios apply. Christ's second coming is now more imminent than ever, and, as Proverbs 15:3 points out, "The eyes of the Lord are everywhere, keeping watch on the wicked and the good." Examining our interactions in light of either God's earthly or eternal nearness will surely help us pick our battles better. And—I can't resist adding—if you want to know who ultimately wins, read Revelation. In the meantime, let's not forget Jesus' bottom-line beatitude in Matthew 5:9—"Blessed are the peacemakers, for they will be called children of God."

Now we come to Philippians 4:6, which outlines a more supernatural scenario for calming our hearts and minds. "Do not be anxious about anything, but in every situation, by prayer and petition, with thanksgiving, present your requests to God."

We all know that prayer relieves pressure simply by allowing us to unburden our hearts. But we might find our prayers even more productive if we note that Paul draws a distinction here between prayer and petition. Aren't they the same? Not really. Petition—asking for something—is only one small part of prayer.

According to the model prayer of Christ found in Matthew 6:9-13 (commonly known as The Lord's Prayer), the proper path toward approaching God begins by first acknowledging God's high holiness, sovereign will, provision, and forgiveness, which also includes our need to forgive others, and divine direction and protection. Surely if we would practice prefacing our petitions this way, they would take on a different perspective.

Undoubtedly that's why Philippians 4:6 also includes thanksgiving as an important part of our prayers. "Gratitude," said the ancient Roman philosopher Cicero, "is not only the greatest of virtues, but the parent of all others." Expressing sincere thanks to God opens yet another door that casts eternal light on everything else we might ask or experience.

Here's how Sarah Ben Breathnach, author of the book *Simple Abundance,* says it: "If you give thanks for five gifts every day, in two months you will look at life differently." As already noted, even in the depths of our worst dilemma, there are blessings, inspirations, and encouragement all around if we'll just train ourselves to take notice.

One great illustration of this gratitude-changing attitude came in the form of an e-mail I received a few years ago around Thanksgiving. It was from Jon Katterhorn, a man I had met at a local writer's conference, and opened with Psalm 75:1—"We give thanks to you, O God, we give thanks, For your Name is near; Men declare Your wondrous works" (NASB).

Jon then proceeded to share a number of wonderful deeds God had done in his life. He ended by writing these words: "I give thanks for the many friendships that I have, that our family walks with the Lord, and that Mom and Dad are doing great. In everything we do let us give thanks."

This could easily be chalked up as just another bit of cheery holiday chatter until I tell you that Jon has lived his entire life severely disabled with cerebral palsy. Now over fifty years old, he struggles painfully to walk and be understood. Yet he lives an amazingly full life, obviously having no trouble communicating to God and others about the things he is thankful for.

Volumes more could be written about the virtues of gratitude—and have been. The question is how to put it into practice. Taken again from the article "Got Gratitude?" the author offers a couple more simple suggestions. First, imagine your life without its blessings. Focusing on how much worse off you would be without the things in your life that make you happy helps you appreciate them more. Second, perform a gratitude swap. When you catch yourself dwelling on the negative, jot down what's bothering you. Then, cross it off, substituting something you're grateful for. "Thinking you deserve better or that life hasn't turned out the way you want," she concludes, "stops you from seeing the positive."

Coming now to Philippians 4:7, Paul offers us the very thing spoken of in our last chapter—one of God's precious promises. "And the peace of God, which transcends all understanding, will guard your hearts and your minds in Christ Jesus."

Is it really possible that a major key to experiencing both spiritual and emotional peace lies merely in applying the preceding principles? It is if the early apostles are any example. Consider for instance the passage in Acts 12:6-7, where we find the apostle Peter imprisoned, awaiting trial. "The night before Herod was to bring him to trial," it says, "Peter was sleeping between two soldiers, bound with two chains, and sentries stood guard at the entrance. Suddenly an angel of the Lord appeared and a light shone in the cell. He struck Peter on the side and woke him up. 'Quick, get up!' he said, and the chains fell off Peter's wrists."

Sort of a stressful time for Peter, wouldn't we say? Yet there's something here I find as amazing as the Lord sending an angel to intervene. It's that despite the pre-celestial circumstances, the angel found Peter so soundly asleep between two guards that he had to poke him awake. If that isn't peace, what is? To me, the real sentries in this situation are the unseen ones Paul previously speaks of—those peacefully guarding Peter's heart and mind.

Coming to Philippians 4:8, Paul approaches the conclusion of this passage by pointing out some specific and practical parts of this positive-thinking process. "Finally, brothers and sisters, whatever is true, whatever is noble, whatever is right, whatever is pure, whatever is lovely, whatever is admirable—if anything is excellent or praiseworthy—think about such things." As a point of clarification here, this particular wording comes from the *New International Version*. While other Bible versions use a variety of synonyms, the meanings carry basically the same connotations. Let's take them one by one.

Whatever is true. In a world where truth has become situation-relative and easily rationalized, how can we hope to determine what is true? It's simple—by comparing everything we encounter to the truths found in God's Word, which according to Psalm 119:160 are both current and unchanging. "All your words are true," David writes; "all your righteous laws are eternal." When everything around us is shifting, only by consistently consulting God's Word can we hope to remain on solid spiritual ground.

Our other measure and model of truth is Christ. Remember not long ago the campaign in Christian circles urging us to consider *What Would Jesus Do?* simply symbolized as *WWJD?* Though some sport (and undoubtedly a bit of profit) was made from all the peripheral paraphernalia, the concept carries serious biblical weight.

According to John 1:14 Jesus *is* the Word [of God] "who became flesh and made his dwelling among us." Jesus himself says in John 8:31, "If you hold to my teaching, you are really my disciples. Then you will know the truth, and the truth will set you free." A little farther along, in John 14:6, Jesus offers Thomas and the other disciples this truth-discovering direction: "I am the way and the truth and the life. No one comes to the Father except through me." So we must always, as Hebrews 12:2 instructs, "fix our eyes on Jesus, the pioneer and perfecter of faith." If we do that, we can't go wrong. And that is the truth.

Whatever is noble. "Noble" is a word we don't hear much anymore, perhaps because few really understand or stop to consider what it means. The dictionary defines it two ways: first as "possessing hereditary rank in a political system or social class" and second, "having or showing qualities of high moral character, such as courage, generosity, honor . . . anything indicative of such a character; showing magnanimity."[4]

I would say in the case of Christians both apply. We are, after all, the heirs of God as indicated in His Word. In case you haven't examined your spiritual birth certificate lately, let me remind you that Romans 8:16-17 tells us, "The Spirit himself testifies with our spirit that we are God's children. Now if we are children, then we are heirs—heirs of God and co-heirs with Christ."

Wouldn't you agree, then, that as King's kids we should be acting a bit more like it, striving to bring honor and glory to Him by seeking the high or regal road in both our thoughts and actions? As Isaiah 32:8 poetically points out: "The noble make noble plans, and by noble deeds they stand." And exactly how does this noble notion translate to real life? James 2:8 leaves little doubt. "If you really keep the royal law found in Scripture, 'Love your neighbor as yourself,' you are doing right." Surely if we could only manage to act more lovingly toward others, all other Kingdom commands could be more easily accomplished. It's also amazing how focusing on the needs of others gives us less time to dwell on our own wants and worries. This leads us, then, to the next part of Paul's admonition.

Whatever is right. Contrary to today's trend toward political correctness, there are still strict biblical standards for right and wrong, good and evil, light and darkness. Unfortunately in our dim world we encounter many shades of gray, making it easy at times to get our facts confused. Even at our spiritual best, we can't rely on our own rationalization. "There is a way that appears to be right," Proverbs 14:12 warns us, "but in the end it leads to death."

In order to know what is truly right, we have to see things as God does. Again, this comes only by reading His Word, then shining its light on every situation. "I have hidden your word in my heart that I might not sin against you," says Psalm 119:11, then later in verse 105: "Your word is a lamp for my feet, a light for my path."

Undoubtedly, when faced with the world's wacky way of thinking, there'll be times when doing the right thing makes us feel like a salmon swimming upstream. That's when another of Paul's admonitions found in 2 Thessalonians 3:13 may help renew our resolve: "As for you, brothers and sisters, never tire of doing what is good." In other words, believers, buck the world's tide and keep swimming.

Whatever is pure. When it comes to purity, we should probably consider not only changing our specs but putting on blinders and ear plugs. Every day we are assaulted with so much visual and verbal sewage that some is bound to seep in around the edges. The real danger, however, is when we open the door. Once our hearts and minds are flooded with filth, we're in trouble.

Impurity, of course, comes in many different forms, but the one most visible in today's society and that so often leads down other deviant paths is pornography. No longer limited only to certain magazines and movies, it enters our homes daily through one form of media or another.

My friends Susan and Arden Schmidt are both family counselors who specialize in helping those addicted to pornography. In a recent seminar they spoke about how quickly people—not just men—can get hooked. It was especially eye-opening to learn that medical studies have shown how just one visual exposure causes an immediate change in brain chemistry, proving that pornography is every bit as addicting as any chemical substance—maybe more so. While chemicals eventually leave your body, lewd images and language never leave your mind.

When it comes to keeping ourselves untainted, here's some advice from a man who, sadly, knew firsthand about the consequences of impure actions. In Psalm 119:9 King David writes, "How can a young person stay on the path of purity? By living according to your word"—and, I might add, not lasciviously lurking on balconies with a pair of binoculars. As an old saying goes, "The first look is an accident, but the second look is sin."

Whatever is lovely. Maybe it's no coincidence that this admonition follows next. What better antidote for avoiding lewdness than focusing our eyes and ears instead on what is lovely? Despite the sad state of many people and places in the world, there is still an abundance of beauty to be found if we will only look for it—even if it's nothing more than a flower growing in the crack of an inner-city sidewalk. Again, it all depends on what we opt to observe. As previously mentioned, it's amazing how seeking out an inspiring change of scenery can open our eyes to fresh ideas, people, and possibilities, giving even old problems new perspective.

Something else that helps when our spirit needs a boost is listening to soothing or spiritually inspiring music. And how about sitting down with a heartwarming book, magazine article, television show, or movie—whatever will leave us feeling uplifted, rested, and restored. For that matter, just sitting in the quiet can sometimes provide the loveliest lift of all.

There may also come a time when we have to look for loveliness in unlikely circumstances. My friend Marla reminded me recently about the terrible fire that almost totally destroyed her brother's home. Though it was one of the worst experiences of their lives, it turned out to be a blessing in disguise. First and foremost, no one was harmed, and most sentimental objects were saved. Second, it allowed them to do a long-postponed-due-to-lack-of-finances home makeover. In the end, beauty truly rose out of ashes—all paid for by insurance. How lovely!

Whatever is admirable. While there are many admiration-worthy objects in life, for me the word most often brings to mind people. And while a lot of people are admired for their looks, ability, or accomplishments, the best kind of people to admire—especially when we're striving to improve our own life outlook—are those who also exhibit these same positive spiritual qualities to which we aspire.

Along those lines, consider something I spotted recently on Facebook. It was written by my respected friend and colleague Joan Smith, who serves as Women's Director for Sacramento Teen Challenge, a life-changing rehabilitation center.

Today I was listening to someone speak about the power of agreement, saying that we need to align ourselves with people who will positively agree with us about important things in our lives. It started me thinking: *Am I surrounding myself with godly men and women who spur me on to righteousness, who agree with me in my service for the Lord, who encourage me to grow in my relationship with God? Or am I aligning myself with people who agree with me in my self-pity, my besetting sins, and so on?*

Joan's conclusion was that the most meaningful mentors in life are those who inspire us to finish our course God's way. And I agree with her, since I know of no one I admire more.

If anything is excellent or praiseworthy. The way this phrase is fitted between dashes toward the end of the text, it's almost as if Paul is saying, "Now if I've left anything out, this should cover it." At the same time, it alludes to not only changing our specs but also lifting our sights—looking beyond the ordinary to the excellent, beyond the everyday to the eternal. "So we fix our eyes not on what is seen," Paul urges in another passage found in 2 Corinthians 4:18, "but on what is unseen, since what is seen is temporary, but what is unseen is eternal." If we are ever to find rest in this weary world, it will be because we finally come to understand how little many of the things we currently lose sleep over matter when illuminated by eternity.

Finally, in reference to everything he has just written, Paul adds this instruction in Philippians 4:8: "Think about such things." Bible scholars concur that the word "think" translated from this passage's original language means more than just quick consideration; rather, these are concepts to be contemplated, reflected on regularly, and weighed until they are so firmly fixed in our minds that they become a natural outgrowth of our everyday existence. No wonder Paul then pushes it one step further.

Whatever you have learned or received or heard from me, or seen in me—put it into practice.

Lest we presume that the apostle is putting himself on a pedestal here, we need only take a closer look at his life. Paul was not preaching anything that he wasn't also personally striving to apply. So all he was actually saying is "Whatever Christlike characteristics you've seen in or learned from me, don't *just* think about them. Start doing them!" Practice does, after all, make perfect.

One of the best "textbooks" I've ever read on applying the same such godly principles is one written by a seventeenth-century French monk named Brother Lawrence. Serving as a mere monastery cook, he made an amazing commitment to live every moment—whether in the kitchen or the cathedral—with an intentional, pervading awareness of God's presence. *The Practice of the*

Presence of God chronicles his personal yet influential journey and has become an inspiring, much-recommended Christian classic.[5]

What about us less-than-priestly people? Is it really possible to change our pessimistic earthly outlooks into more positive heavenly ones? I believe one last testimony taken from an online article by my missionary friend Lynne Chandler will adequately address both issues, also allowing us to see that even those committed to ministry must work to correct near-sightedness. Lynne wrote—

When we first arrived in Croatia, I did not like living there. I complained to God about every challenge and difficulty I encountered. Finally, one day [in prayer] the Holy Spirit seemed to respond, *Why can't you just enjoy the ride?*

I don't believe the Lord was being harsh or trying to put me through an endurance test. But He wanted me to see with my spiritual eyes all that He was trying to do in my life. He wanted me to *enjoy* His process of teaching me to depend on Him and His power *now*, not just get by, barely surviving each day.

After the Holy Spirit spoke to me, I did learn to enjoy the ride. It was difficult at first because I was fearful and had developed a negative and complaining spirit. But I purposed to change my attitude, and over time things began to change. Croatia has become my favorite place to live and minister, which shows that even stubborn people like me can adjust and be transformed. I have found so many hidden treasures and personal victories in my spiritual walk with the Lord in the middle of difficult seasons, storms, and uncertainties.

Recently, I came upon a quote that describes my new purpose and how I want to enter heaven: "Life is not a journey to the grave with intentions of arriving safely . . .

but rather to skid in broadside, thoroughly used up, totally worn out and loudly proclaiming, 'WOW! What a ride!'"[6]

Perhaps to some, Lynne's last line sounds anything but restful until we realize how joyfully it rings with renewed interest and energy—the kind that only a purposeful and positive outlook on life can produce.

Therefore I submit that by swapping our spiritual specs—learning to look for God's best rather than the world's worst—we will be changing not only our general attitude but our "sabbatitude" as well. How? The more we focus on these and other spiritual specifics, the less earthly convolution and pollution will influence us. The more our spiritual vision sharpens, the clearer our choices become, freeing our minds from confusion and consequently from worry.

No wonder, then, that Paul finishes the passage with "And the God of peace will be with you" (verse 9). That phrase alone is a salve for sore eyes.

❖ 11 ❖
PLANNING A PERSONAL SABBATH

*There remains, then, a Sabbath-rest for the people of
God; for anyone who enters God's rest also rests from
their own works, just as God did from his. Let us,
therefore, make every effort to enter that rest. . . ."*
—Hebrews 4:9-11

Well, since that introductory lap around my local park, we've
logged a few literary miles. So far our journey has covered everything from Creation to corrective spiritual lenses with stops
at Mt. Sinai and some pertinent (I hope) points in between.
My prayer is that along the way we've collected a keepsake or
two—not the least of which is a better understanding of both
the religious and restorative reasons for seeking Sabbath rest.
Now we arrive at an important crossroad: deciding how we'll
incorporate all the information we've acquired. According to
our above theme scripture, Sabbath rest still remains available
to us, but entering into it will require some ongoing effort.

"Effort," to summarize one dictionary definition, "is an attempt, great or small, to do something . . . usually implying a
substantial expenditure of time, strength, or faculties."[1] Seems

counterintuitive, doesn't it, to think that rest might require work? But it's true. Like everything worthwhile in life, the Sabbath associations and resources shared throughout this book aren't going to automatically or immediately implement themselves. That is unless we finally exhaust ourselves into a dead faint—which I fear many of us are calamitously close to doing.

Let me see if I can soften the concept a little. What effort really amounts to is first making a mental commitment, then physically following through. Much easier, right?

Right.

Perhaps, then, it's finally time to use a few pages for laying out some specifics of implementing a personal Sabbath. Before we break out the blueprints, however, let me squeeze in one more foundational formula received from someone much admired for his practical, purposeful teaching. Though it may smack of previously trodden trails, I believe it offers some fresh perspective.

The person I'm speaking of is Rick Warren, nationally recognized pastor and author of *The Purpose Driven Life*. A few years ago my husband and I had the privilege of hearing Rick share with a group of pastors on the subject of Sabbath rest. Since he oversees a church with satellite congregations totaling more than fifteen thousand members, we figured the good reverend might have some significant insights. Here is the pithy but pertinent three-part counsel he offered:

- Divert daily
- Withdraw weekly
- Abandon annually

The way Rick defined daily diversion is to find a time every day for doing something completely different from our occupation. For instance, those who work with their minds might find a way of relaxing with their hands, perhaps taking up a hobby like crafting or carpentry. Conversely, those who do manual labor might sample something more mind-challenging, such as reading, completing crossword puzzles, even taking a class, online or otherwise. The point is to make an *effort* every day to do something that offers a complete diversion, thus a true transition.

When it comes to weekly withdrawal, Rick reiterated both the biblical statute and benefits of religiously setting aside an entire day every week, making it a true Sabbath by incorporating worship, rest, and recreation. While the constitutional elements of Sabbath have already been explored and elaborated in a previous chapter, let me just highlight one thing. Contrary to conventional thinking, Sabbath celebration doesn't mean we're restricted to sit and twiddle our spiritual thumbs. It does, however, mean keeping rest and reverence at the top of the priority list and making sure whatever else we do glorifies God with our entire being—mind, body, and spirit. But, then, shouldn't we be doing that every day?

"For pastors," Rick reemphasized, "this has to be a day other than Sunday." Truth is, everyone might benefit from occasionally spending a day off in addition to Sunday, even if it means taking some vacation time from work.

Here's another idea. How about considering a Sabbath from social media? Ever consider that "retweeting" from Twitter and backing off Facebook might help us realize just how much of our daily stress is actually due to information overload and the pressure to stay constantly connected, thus always on call? I have some friends who recently "fasted" from all electronic media for an entire week. And they didn't die. Quite the opposite, according to them the extended exit from all that influx of information not only worked restful wonders but also opened up more actual face-time with family and friends.

The same could be said of scheduling a day away from worry. Face it. No matter how hard we try not to let our worries overwhelm us, there will be days when it proves humanly impossible. Those are the days when I've actually said out loud, "Okay, Lord. I'm sick of stressing over this. I'm taking a day off." Sounds silly, I suppose, but there's something psychological about declaring a Sabbath from stress whereby for twenty-four hours we refuse to entertain any anxious thoughts. Of course, it would help even more if we fill the void with some instruction found in Psalm 46:10: "Be still, and know that I am God." Perhaps if we implemented this kind of Sabbath more often, our worries would eventually take an extended vacation.

This brings us back to Rick's admonition about abandoning annually, which simply means scheduling a vacation every year that temporarily relocates us from our place of work, ministry, and regular routine. My only additional suggestion—gleaned from exasperating experience—is to make sure we don't counteract the retreating benefits by overscheduling, overspending, or traveling so far we don't leave adequate time for unwinding. Though our minds may comprehend that we are on vacation, our bodies often require a few days to catch up, or vice-versa. In the case of family vacations, also keep in mind that—though *they* may not think so—kids need down time too. The same goes for our marriages. There's nothing wrong with occasionally calling on Grandma and then careening away kid-less.

We might even consider staying close to home. Just don't tell anyone. One of the best weeks away my husband and I have ever taken was at a lovely church-sponsored vacation home about three hours from where we live, near the ocean. Not only was there no time adjustment, but also everything we needed was provided, and the beach and browsing areas were within easy walking distance. We made one short food foray and then snuggled in, cooking many of our own super-simple meals. For the entire week we decided on a daily, sometimes hourly, basis what we wanted to do—or not. One day we adventurously broke out some bicycles. Luckily that's all we broke. It was awesome.

Frankly, I was amazed my husband took so readily to it. Usually his type-A tendencies make it hard for him not to set schedules even on free time. What helped—in addition to the fact that he was thoroughly exhausted—is that we had made an agreement beforehand to give each other two hours after breakfast for writing (me) and checking e-mail (him); then the rest of the day was to be ours together—unwired.

Sad, isn't it? Some of us actually have to force ourselves to stop imposing schedules and perfectionism even on the fun things we do. This reminds me of something I observed when speaking at a recent women's retreat. Hoping to encourage fellowship and interaction, the planners had provided some board games for the gals to enjoy during their free time. Almost immediately following our first gathering, one group quickly spread out a giant jigsaw puzzle. Fun and relaxing, right? Yes, except they were soon so into it that they couldn't quit. Long after the last person headed for bed, they kept working. Some of us even joked about coming in the next morning and finding them face down on the table with puzzle pieces stuck to their faces. Turns out, it wasn't far from the truth. These dear ladies became so determined to finish that puzzle that they spent every spare moment on it. Even on the last day as people were packing for home, they were fitting in the last few pieces.

In their defense, I know they found both the challenge and fellowship enjoyable. Still, there's something to be said, especially for us perfectionist types, about packing only projects that can be easily picked up and put down, leaving our completion compulsion at home.

This also illustrates the hardest initial part of any real effort at rest and retreat—be it daily, weekly, or longer. That is simply to gear down. Let me share another little story excerpted from an article written by my friend Jodie Detrick that I believe will offer some encouragement.

On May 25, 2008, after traveling four hundred twenty-two million miles from earth to the northern polar region of Mars, the *Phoenix Mars Lander* made a near-perfect landing. That alone is amazing, but here's another little-known fact. In order to execute a "soft" landing on the Red Planet's dusty surface, the Lander had to decrease its speed from twelve thousand five hundred to five miles per hour within *seven* minutes of piercing the Martian atmosphere.

For this to happen, it took some major engineering effort. The parachute had to deploy at just the right time; the reverse engine thrusters had to kick in to slow down the free-fall, and the craft had to make self-adjustments to right itself for a level landing. See any personal parallels here?

The good news is that if something as humongous as the *Phoenix Mars Lander* can go from twelve thousand five hundred to five miles per hour in only seven minutes, we can too. Still, Jodie pegged it when she added, "Obviously great care and planning were necessary to go from whizzing through space down to a manageable five miles per hour. I suspect it will take similar planning for us too." Again, that is where the effort comes in. Not only must we pre-program but we must also *re*-program.

Another difficult thing, no matter how careful our calculations, is to avoid packing our problems along. A humorous illustration of this comes from the archives of our afore-mentioned friend and mentor Glen Cole. He often told the story of a mother who came home one day to find her seven children hunched into a circle in the middle of the living room floor. Something in the center had obviously captured their attention. Peeking into the pack, the mom made a horrific discovery: seven baby skunks. "Run children, run!" she screamed in panic. So every kid grabbed a skunk and ran. The obvious moral of the story is that when we truly want to escape a stressful situation, we shouldn't take our "skunks" with us.

"Learning to ignore things," wrote author Robert J. Sawyer, "is one of the great paths to inner peace"—and, may I add, one of the hardest things for most of us to accomplish. Yet undoubtedly the biggest key to making any personal Sabbath—or ordinary day, for that matter—successful is finding some way to release the things we find distracting or distressing.

At the same time, it's often not until we settle into an atmosphere of relaxation and reflection that stressful, long-stuffed thoughts begin to surface. Somehow, like scum on the water, we must find a healthy method for skimming them off. Pray, cry, talk to a trusted friend. Do whatever is necessary to release those rest-robbing emotions. Then sit patiently in God's presence. Once the stress drains out, it leaves an empty reservoir into which He can begin to pour healing, restoration, and resolution.

Sometimes we're surprised to discover how stressed out we've been. A few years ago my good friend Sherilyn was serendipitously treated to a spa treatment. After an amazing massage, she was sitting in the "relaxing room" with an accompanying group of friends when suddenly an unexpected, unstoppable torrent of tears began to fall. Seeing the concern on her spa sisters' faces, she finally managed to snuffle out, "I feel so good. Why can't I stop crying?"

The underlying truth was that Sherilyn had just recently said good-bye to one of her sons and family who were moving cross-country. Not wanting to show up puffy-eyed later that morning at a church event, she had held her emotions in. Unknowingly, Sherilyn had just answered her own question. Often it's not until we begin to feel better that we realize how bad we felt before.

A few times a year I, too, have the privilege of joining a group of friends for a delicious day of personal pampering. On one such spa spree we were surprised before being taken in for our treatments to be handed a piece of thick twine. Our instructions were to take a few quiet minutes and think of everything that was currently causing stress in our lives, then tie a knot in the twine representing each. After we had done so, we were to leave our pieces of twine in a bowl outside the treatment area. Proverbially speaking, we were dropping our worries at the door. Lo and behold, by the time we returned, they had "miraculously" disappeared.

Now I ask you. What if during our times alone with the Lord we did the same symbolic thing? I can tell you from experience that the miracle He performs when untangling our knotted nerves will go way beyond mere imagination.

Of course, like a good massage, the residual effects from times of retreat never last long enough to permanently protect us from stress. Eventually we have to go back to the real world. What it does accomplish, though, is to interrupt the pain and pressure long enough to provide a reprieve and a release. That is why we must make the effort to do it often.

From my friend Jodie's treasure trove of life-coach counsel, let me share one more simple retreat format:

- Get away.
- Go alone (or with a close companion).
- Rest well.
- Listen closely.
- Produce nothing.

Perhaps when it comes to implementing Sabbath rest, our biggest "sabbatitude" step is accepting the idea that God is not assigning penance but giving us permission. For what? To temporarily put everything aside and through rest and reflection allow Him to massage our tired physical and spiritual muscles. Sadly, it's something we don't always permit ourselves to do.

That's why, like the Israelites, we must be reminded often. In Exodus 16:29-30, long-suffering Moses once again states the obvious: "'Bear in mind that the LORD has given you the Sabbath; that is why on the sixth day he gives you bread for two days. Everyone is to stay where he is on the seventh day; no one is to go out.' So the people rested on the seventh day."

There remains a Sabbath day of rest. God tries to make it easy for us. But in the end, we are the ones who must make every effort to pick up and implement what He has provided.

❖ 12 ❖
Planning the "Perfect" Sabbatical

In their hearts humans plan their course,
but the LORD establishes their steps.
—Proverbs 16:9

Now it's time to pull out the big blueprints. As beneficial and necessary as any regular Sabbath may be, there will undoubtedly come a time—or ten—in every life when we wake up one morning realizing that taking an hour a day, one day a week, or even an annual vacation just isn't cutting it. It's time to consider a full-fledged sabbatical.

As a spring-board reminder, let me offer a shortened version of the sabbatical definition given in the introductory chapter: "a leave, often with pay granted . . . usually every seventh year." In reality, of course, taking a sabbatical every seven years is for most of us quite unlikely. Not that we wouldn't want to, but not all employers provide time or pay for it, and few of us can personally afford one that frequently.

Still, the concept of an every-seventh-year sabbatical has very literal scriptural roots and for good reason. As part of a long list of laws God gave to Moses, Exodus 23:10-11 says, "For six years you are to sow your fields and harvest the crops, but during the seventh year let the land lie unplowed and unused." In all probability, this law was issued as much for the benefit of the land as it was for the Israelites, since overworking the ground takes all the nutrients out of it—a lesson hard-learned by Americans during the Dustbowl of the early 1930s. Due to the depleted dirt, soon crops wouldn't grow; consequently, there was nothing to hold the soil in place, resulting in dust storms of diabolic magnitude.

The same thing sometimes happens to people. Only in our case, overwork can result in having nothing left to hold the *soul* in place. It's commonly called *burn-out*. Consequently—though there are many more positive reasons for planning a sabbatical—it's no surprise that often the decision coincides with circumstances revolving around significant emotional or physical distress or transition, times when we're desperately in need of extended time to reflect, regroup, and repurpose. In severe cases, a sabbatical may be the only hope of bringing our lives and emotions back into balance—hopefully before we've attempted too many other less-than-satisfactory antidotes; or, worse, made major mistakes.

It's not unusual, either, for people to wait until the middle or later years of life to plan sabbaticals. Most commonly, that's because it takes that long for us to feel we've finally earned it. Also, at mid-life some of us suddenly become aware that there may be a drastic difference between achieving success and experiencing satisfaction or significance—and how little time we have left to do it. Ironically, time is exactly what we need to sort it all out.

All this to say that there is really no set or perfect scenario for taking a sabbatical, yet for any number of reasons, it's something we should all pursue at one time or another. So with that in mind, what does an actual sabbatical look like? The way I would like to address that is two-fold.

First, since covering every sabbatical variation and aspect would require another entire book, I'll initially offer just a few general observations. Second, I would like to end the chapter by sharing some snapshots from our own sabbatical album, using them to illustrate personal insights that might give guidance. I will admit right now that while there are many things we did right, there are others we would definitely do differently if given the opportunity. Perhaps between the two, a useful selection of sabbatical ideas will surface.

I also suggest that a wise part of sabbatical preparation would be to speak with others who have taken one. Though undoubtedly many different opinions and impressions will surface, some good suggestions and insights will surely be gleaned.

So here we go.

When it comes to the appropriate length of time for a sabbatical, there is really nothing set in stone. It should, however, constitute more than an extended vacation, both in perimeter and purpose. Most would say that nothing less than six weeks would qualify. I spoke recently with one minister's wife who told me she and her husband had just taken a month-long sabbatical, then proceeded to describe how many times they came home to participate in "unavoidable" family and ministry functions. Not only was this *not* a sabbatical, but it also wasn't even a good vacation.

As a general rule, most sabbaticals last two to six months and some for an entire year, depending on the person and particulars. Educators, for example, are often granted up to a year's leave of absence for the purpose of extended study or writing. At the very least, a sabbatical should serve to get us off life's roller coaster long enough to break the destructive, unproductive patterns of stress that we all unavoidably develop. At best, it should provide enough uninterrupted time to adequately assess things in our lives that may be hindering true productivity or the pursuit of long-deferred dreams. This means going someplace for at least part of the time where people and pressures can't easily find you. That's tough to do in today's techo-connected world—I know.

I suppose some who take sabbaticals later in life might view it as a practice run for retirement. In that respect, one of the benefits of time away from the everyday stuff of life is that it reveals how much we might yet wish to accomplish—and how little might actually be needed to do it. It struck me that when the Israelites were commanded to let the ground rest from planting (sort of a temporary retirement, couldn't we say?), it didn't turn entirely to weeds. In fact, what grew voluntarily during this dormant period was still enough to feed them, their animals, and the servants. Likewise, it might be delightful to discover how much emotional nourishment we can derive simply from what serendipitously sprouts during a sabbatical off-season—or how resourceful we can be with whatever presents itself.

At the same time, being on sabbatical doesn't mean we can't be productive. Some people, in fact, use the time to do things they wouldn't be able to do under everyday circumstances, responsibilities, and pressures—travel, write a book, take a class, make a spiritual pilgrimage. Either way, we shouldn't be surprised if things attempted and accomplished on sabbatical lead to the eventual opening of an entirely new chapter in life. In the end, that's perhaps the best by-product of all.

I suppose it goes without saying—but I'll say it anyway—that in order for a sabbatical to provide spiritual enrichment, it must have a "God" component, even if that means merely incorporating a good daily devotional, then taking time for prayer and meditation. There are sabbaticals, of course, taken for the sole purpose of seeking an in-depth spiritual experience. My friend Marla's time away from her seminary teaching position revolved around a personal interest in the origins and principles behind planning silent spiritual retreats. This included spending six months overseas, observing and studying the models of a number of missionaries, missions, and monasteries.

Obviously a successful sabbatical is not something that should be started "spur of the moment." In truth, the kind of planning required takes the word *effort* to a whole new level. Let me give you just a glimpse.

First there are the logistics: Where to go, how long to stay, travel and accommodation reservations both en route and after arrival, putting aside adequate savings to fund the entire trip, arranging for someone to handle house care, mail-gathering and bill-paying in absentia (though granted, electronic bill-paying has taken some of the trouble out of that)—and the list goes on. Depending on our design and destination(s), that is just the tip of the iceberg. The point is that careful preparation and planning are the best way to ensure that once we depart, everything will (hopefully) fall into place, resulting in a truly restful and rewarding experience.

The bottom line is that a sabbatical must be custom-made for every individual and situation. In order to truly provide rest, it should incorporate some reasonable limitations. For instance, because my husband is not only a minister but a denominational executive responsible for the often-exhausting oversight of four hundred fifty churches, our presbytery gave instructions that during our sabbatical there should be no formal ministry scheduled. True confession: we fudged a few times on that, but only because we were offered some once-in-a-lifetime opportunities that we found irresistible and truly enjoyable.

That brings me, then, to the personal sabbatical observations I want to share. As hard as it is for me to believe, it has now been exactly three years since in late October we boarded a jumbo jet that propelled us on the first leg of our long-anticipated sabbatical journey. As mentioned in my introductory chapter, our basic plan—after saving for more than a year—was to take two months off, beginning with a week revisiting our Midwestern roots, then on to Europe, and finally back home.

Thus, the first lap found us flying from Sacramento, California, to St. Louis, Missouri, which sits just across the mighty Mississippi River from my husband's adorably quaint hometown in southern Illinois. Finding the entire area dressed in its fall finest, we leaf-kicked our way through the first few unstructured days exploring, revisiting, and reminiscing. This included a short car trip to Springfield, Missouri, where Jim was to be honored as an "alumni of the year" by our alma mater, Central Bible College. As part of the ceremony, he was scheduled to speak in chapel—the first of our aforementioned "fudges."

Here's my first insight. Though this was all part of our original plan, I believe the fact that it came at the very beginning was providential in that it offered us a true and meaningful time of transition. Not only was it a great week of reconnecting with our historical and biological roots, but it was also a sentimental refocusing of the place where our journey of marriage and ministry started.

We spent time with long-lost friends and seldom-seen family, those who knew us "when" and with whom we had shared significant early-life experiences. A special video presentation during the college ceremony, featuring a personal photo biography, served as a visual reminder of all that had transpired in the years between. It was a true nostalgia trip but also helped us recall our humble beginnings—not a bad sabbatical springboard.

The next leg of our journey reconnected us with some other lifelong friends, not to mention our more far-reaching foreign roots. So it was that after driving back to St. Louis, we boarded a plane for Berlin. There we were met by former college friends, now missionaries, John and Gayle Butrin. This was a deliberate choice for two reasons. First, both Jim's and my maternal families immigrated from Germany; second, we knew the Butrins were laid-back enough to let us really rest.

At the same time, I also knew my husband would never really relax without a bit of "debriefing." Eager to hear all the happenings at home, John was just the guy to accommodate him. To be on the safe side, however, I imposed a twenty-four-hour time limit for office talk. Then it was on to R&R.

For the next ten days we basically slept, explored Berlin's autumn ambience, and ate good German food. In the process, we relived a little history, having the good fortune to arrive just in time for the twenty-year celebration of the fall of the East-West wall. Though this meant standing for five hours at the famous Brandenburg Gate with several thousand people in a chilling fall drizzle, we wouldn't have missed the experience for the world.

Other historical and educational day trips included visiting Wittenburg, where Martin Luther nailed his ninety-five famous Reformation theses to the church door, and Potsdam, a picturesque German town most famous for a World War II treaty signed there. In between we rested and de-stressed, cocooned within the amazing architecture of the Butrins' one-hundred-year-old flat, which Gayle had creatively and gorgeously furnished.

Through the Butrins' unique ministry of friendship evangelism, we also met some fun and fascinating people—none connected to our "other" life. From this came my one and only "fudge": accepting Gayle's gracious invitation to speak for

Christian Women of Berlin, an international group embracing those from every faith.

Here's my second insight. Though we had traveled several thousand miles, the change of scenery and enjoyable cultural connections caused us hardly to notice the jet lag. In fact, we felt exhilarated. The observation here is that busyness without the daily stress or personal responsibility can actually constitute a different kind of rest. Much of this, of course, depends on picking the right places to go and people to relax with or, in some cases, not spending time with people at all. For us, the opportunity to enjoy good friends' hospitality versus staying in a strange hotel was infinitely more appealing.

The next part of our itinerary took us to Dublin—a place where we hoped to retrace a footprint or two from Jim's paternal side of the family. We had planned to meet another set of long-time friends, Dan and Kathy Stump, there. As missionaries in Barcelona, Spain, the Stumps' multiple years of ministry throughout Europe, not to mention their fun-loving personalities, make them ideal traveling companions.

Unfortunately, while still in Berlin we received word that they wouldn't be able to meet us after all. Only a few weeks prior, Dan had experienced a freak accident involving a head injury. Though they he was recuperating well, in the end he required surgery, and his doctor would not release him to fly.

Understandably, Kathy didn't want to come by herself. But since the arrangements were already made, Jim and I saw no reason not to go it alone. Little did we know.

Arriving at the Dublin airport, we picked up a rental car, whereupon Jim took on the daunting task of learning to drive on the left side of the road—a responsibility we previously planned to share. He wasn't too worried about it until he discovered that *everything* in the car—seats, steering wheel, gages and gears (yes, it was a stick shift to boot)—was the reverse of what he was familiar with.

Add to that the strange roads and roundabouts, these latter being circular intersections that if you miss your exit, keep you perpetually driving 'round about—which we did several times. Consequently, it was after dark when we finally arrived at our first bed and breakfast inn and fell thankfully into bed.

The next morning, at our innkeeper's suggestion, we took a less stressful mode of transportation, hopping a train into downtown Dublin. There we managed a few hours of concentrated sightseeing before returning to pick up our car and head south to the coastal town of Cork. Wanting to spend the week exploring as much as possible, we hadn't allowed ourselves much leeway. By the time we maneuvered a few more roundabouts and cruised into Cork, it was dark again. On top of that, the weather had taken a rainy turn.

Still, not to shame our ancestors and be put off by a fine Irish mist, morning found us climbing to the top of nearby Blarney Castle just so Jim could kiss the famous stone. Purportedly this bestows the busser with the gift of gab—as if he really needed that. Afterward we caught the ferry to Cobh (pronounced "Cove"), where we visited an Irish immigration museum and enjoyed lunch.

Emerging, we discovered that the mist had turned into a full-on drizzle, so we decided to make a mad dash to our next scheduled stop—the Dingle Peninsula. On the way, unfortunately, the weather deteriorated rapidly. Five weary, road-winding hours later, we were blown into Dingle City by gale-force winds and a driving rain.

As we woke to yet another wet and windy day, it finally occurred to us that we might check the far-sighted forecast before continuing our pre-planned itinerary to the west. That's when we discovered that parts of Ireland and the entire United Kingdom were experiencing some of the worst flooding in years. The only sane decision was to make a beeline back toward Dublin, fortunately finagling reservations at the same bed and breakfast inn where we stayed our first night.

So from Ireland's shamrock-y shores comes another set of insights. Even with the best planning, things are bound to happen that we can't control. Likewise, it's possible we might make a wrong turn—or three. That's when it's important just to step back, take a deep breath, and look for a logical alternative. As Jim and I learned, it pays to go with the flow—even though we had no idea how literally that would play out.

Should someone surmise that the week was wasted, let me assure you that we laughed more on this leg of the journey than any of the rest—a good sign that we were still somehow managing to relax. Despite the rain, we saw some of the most gorgeous country and met the most delightful people on the face of the earth. Ironically, the lessons learned and memories made navigating that unnaturally wet week together stand out as some of the best taken from our time away.

As Irish luck would have it, our last day in Dublin dawned fair, allowing us several more hours to snoop before heading to the airport for our last European lap. That evening we landed in Barcelona where we finally hooked up with Dan and Kathy. What fun we had filling them in on all the adventure they missed!

Thankfully, the rain in Spain did *not* fall mainly on the plain, allowing us several sunny days to tour Barcelona's seaside beauty. Dan and Kathy then accompanied us to Madrid, where we met with other Spain-based missionaries for an annual two-day retreat. This included a traditional Thanksgiving dinner (yay—American food!) and Jim's second "fudge," in the form of offering a short devotional.

The following Sunday, he spoke one last time at the International Church of Barcelona, where Dan and Kathy serve as pastors. In both situations, our rationalization was that since he was wearing casual clothes and sitting on a stool, it didn't qualify as real preaching—simply *sharing*.

One interesting side note here is that while visiting the church we met an entire family on sabbatical. The parents had decided that it would be worth homeschooling their children for an entire year in order to give them a cross-cultural experience. For those who can arrange and afford it, it's something worth considering.

Another point worth reemphasizing is that regardless of well-intentioned restrictions, it simply may not be possible while on sabbatical to entirely disengage from our occupations, especially the parts we find enjoyable. I don't believe we should condemn ourselves for that. After all, what's the point of taking a sabbatical and then going on a guilt trip?

We should, however, avoid anything smacking of occupational stress. It was also during our time in Barcelona that Jim received an e-mail from a disgruntled, rather demanding pastor, which, with permission, I quickly intercepted and rerouted to a capable colleague back home for response and resolution.

Speaking of home, during our time abroad we did occasionally communicate by e-mail with both Jim's office and our family, just to assure and be assured that everyone was okay. Thankfully, there were no real emergencies. In fact, we felt slightly chagrined to learn that life went right on without us. Somehow people managed and problems got solved. Go figure.

Still, the time inevitably came when we found ourselves missing the familiar faces and places. Therefore, when at November's end we finally boarded our homebound plane, we were both more than ready to snuggle into our final month stateside.

This included one short early-December detour to San Antonio, where we joined a national group of fellow officials for a fun annual get-together.

The majority of the month, however, was spent decorating for Christmas (something, due to book deadlines, I hadn't done full-out in several years), sitting by our fireplace, and anticipating an after-Christmas visit from all our kids and grands. This proved to be one of our best times together ever and a good way to transition back into real life.

Once the kids were gone, reality set in. We had only a few days of sabbatical left before, as Jim described it, "We have to jump back on the running horse." This gave us time to reflect on all that had transpired. Though we agreed that overall the experience had been both beneficial and enjoyable, there were already a few things we knew we would want to do differently.

First, though it's appealing to get as far from everyday responsibilities as possible and experience other cultures, it might have been more restful and less expensive to have picked a place closer to home. If we did choose Europe again, we would opt not to travel as extensively once we arrived. We decided it would be better to pick one destination and then take local side trips.

Then, of course, there are better months than November for traveling, both weather-wise and holiday-wise. In the case of our schedule, this time of year was the only option. And aside from the unexpected Irish deluge, I personally enjoyed the fall ambience in all our destinations. Those who are not cool weather aficionados, however, should consider either a different time of year or a warmer climate.

Finally, regardless of when, where, and how you travel, it pays to remember that these days everything involved in it is both more expensive and stressful due to airline costs/cutbacks and stricter security measures. Fortunately for us, our only exasperating experience was when, for reasons known only to our airline carrier, they chose to fly us back to the United States on a much smaller jet than customary. This meant we had to make an unscheduled East Coast stop for refueling—an announcement that was rather disconcerting to receive while flying over an ocean. It also caused many of us to miss our next connection.

On a more positive note, let me share what in my opinion was the most beneficial thing we did on our sabbatical. Before we left, I bought both of us a personal journal. My main intention was for these to serve as travelogues that would help us retain and relive our sabbatical memories. Somewhere in the middle of Ireland, my husband suggested we read to each other what we had so far recorded.

Expecting mainly to hear Jim recite the scenic and historical high points, imagine my surprise to discover my usually-stoic husband's musings much more sentimental and introspective than mine. Woven into his words about our wanderings were some endearing ones about me, as well as his concerns about some of the challenges we are facing in our current stage of life. In those few days Jim shared his thoughts and dreams more deeply than he had in the last several years.

What this tells me is that in the stress of everyday life we don't always let our guard down often enough to examine, much less express, our true feelings. Needless to say, this did wonders for rekindling our romance and relationship as well as opening a new dialogue about our future hopes and plans. Whether on sabbatical or not, I highly recommend journaling. There's something about putting things down on paper that bring both release and a sometimes surprising perspective. It seems Jim thought so, too, since it was something he continued to do even after we returned home.

Oh, and one more suggestion: Don't wait forty-three years to tell someone how you really feel about him or her.

Of course, we also set some goals while on sabbatical, like not going back to being so immersed and stressed out in everyday living, nor getting caught up in the constant mode of decision-making and conflict resolution, nor allowing any project or person to entirely deplete our store of energy or resources.

Instead, we pledged to maintain a more balanced life that would allow us to be productive but not lose focus on what's most important. Obviously this means being more intentional about rest and relationships. To prove his personal commitment to that, Jim's Christmas gift to me that year was the promise of a monthly date night.

So have we managed to keep these commitments? Not—to be honest—as consistently as we had hoped, but much more often than we did before. Realistically we both knew that we would never completely be able to avoid deadlines. I'm a writer, after all. But we do strive now, when any kind of commitment or deadline demands extra hours and energy, to take time off during or afterward to recuperate. The most important thing is not to let life become a series of unbroken deadlines. The best way to do that is to keep reminding ourselves that not everything in life is as essential or important as we think.

Hopefullly the "sabbatitudes" that sprang from our sabbatical are pretty obvious. There is one more, though, that overrides all and provides the best incentive for keeping the rest. That is taking time daily to realize how good God has been to us and how many blessings He imparts. Resting in that knowledge is as close to the perfect sabbatical as any of us will ever get.

COMING TO A PEACEFUL CONCLUSION

Then we will not turn away from you;
revive us, and we will call on your name.
—Psalm 80:18

As I start this book's concluding chapter, it's once again the week between Christmas and New Year. This morning the park across the street lies quiet. It is cold enough that a thick frost glazes the grass even as a misty fog rises from the ground. Between the horizon and stippled gray cloud cover a wide strip of early winter sunlight casts its gold-white glow, bathing the bare branches of the trees that stand in dark contrast.

The landscape looks so serene that a few minutes ago, still in my robe and slippers, I grabbed my camera and dashed across the street. *Crazy lady,* I imagined some over-observant neighbor saying. No matter. Something compelled me to capture that mellow moment before it dissolved in the day's warmth. Now downloaded onto my computer screen, that peaceful picture serves as this chapter's inspiration.

It strikes me that this scene is very different from the one in my introductory chapter describing the frenetic, tearful trek I once took around that same park. It might even leave the impression that while I've been writing this book life has settled down, stress has flown out the window, and photo-taking is now my main pastime.

It is true that a few things have flown out the window. But that's because several others hit the fan. The truth is that the time I have spent writing has been as stressful as any other I've ever experienced. In addition to our ongoing effort to balance the potentially all-consuming amount of time and travel attached to Jim's executive position, we've faced some serious family challenges—several of them culminating about this time last year.

Somewhere in the blur my original book deadline also flew right by. Though my editors graciously granted an extension, the frustrating writer's block and insomnia that followed soon made me realize that it just wasn't going to happen. "This is ridiculous," I remember saying to my husband during one period of wee-hour wakefulness. "I'm losing sleep while writing about rest." It was as if everything I had been sanctimoniously cackling about had come home to roost.

That's when I knew an important opportunity had presented itself. It was time for me to test my testimony by stepping back to focus on the more important matters at hand, not the least of which was my mental health. This meant telling my editors that I wouldn't be able to meet even my extended deadline.

I would like to tell you that I easily passed that test, kept calm, and carried on. But I can't. What followed were some maudlin moments. Feeling that I had let both myself and my publisher down, wondering if all the hours I spent praying, thinking, and writing would come to nothing, grieving to think that my words might not see the printer's ink—never mind the light of day—even at one point sinking so low as to ponder how spiritually effective my life has been.

Pathetic, huh, for one so Sabbath savvy? Finally God managed to gently pry my fingers loose, reminding me that this was His book, not mine—meaning the timing, too, belonged to Him.

Surely it was no coincidence that during the same timeframe I received the phone call informing me that our friend Shirley Hawkins, the lighthearted lady I wrote about in a previous chapter who was by then in a nursing home, was near death. I headed over to see her, hoping to lift both our spirits.

And it worked.

As I held her hand and we sang a few beloved hymns, the Lord opened my eyes to see that she represented only one of the many people whose lives we've touched throughout the years and who in turn have touched ours. The fact that Shirley would within a matter of mere days or hours enter her heavenly rest was in small part because we had been privileged to serve as her pastors.

That's when—like this morning's winter sunrise—something serenely significant dawned in my heart. Making room in our lives for rest is ultimately about pursuing peace. It is about taking time on earth for what eternally matters. That way we don't end up looking back on our lives with regret, wishing we had invested more time in the important things and people.

It was well-known author Harriet Beecher Stowe who wrote, "The bitterest tears shed over graves are for words left unsaid and deeds left undone," or as another anonymous person put it, "I never heard of anyone on his or her deathbed saying, 'Man, I wish I had spent more time at the office.'"

Of course, the time I was taking off was time I didn't think I had. Isn't it always? But believe it or not, while writing this book, I've absorbed a thing or two as well, the most important of which is that my relationship with God and the people I love must always come before my personal plans.

I love the poignant way author Max Lucado put it: "When you are in the final days of your life, what will you want? Will you hug that college degree in the walnut frame? Will you ask to be carried to the garage so you can sit in your car? Will you find comfort in rereading your financial statement? Of course not. What will matter then will be people. If relationships will matter most then, shouldn't they matter most now?"

So for those who might have been hoping the final pages of this book would promise that by applying all the preceding principles, life will become less stressful and taking time off more automatic, I have to disappoint. Fact is, if we keep waiting for the stress in our lives to straighten out so we can rest, we'll be waiting forever.

But I can promise you this. Though we may never live stress-free lives, Sabbath rest is always within reach. Though life will not always be peaceful, our hearts can always be at peace—that is, if we finally come to understand that it is not about rowing harder or bailing faster but about simply stopping. Then we can listen closely for Christ's storm-calming words: "Peace, be still."

Speaking of storms makes me think it hasn't been the easiest year (2012) in our country either. From Hurricane Sandy to Sandy Hook Elementary School, some diabolically devastating things happened—things from which we'll be reeling for a long time. And though I hate to say it, Scripture indicates that world conditions may not improve much either. If they don't, what will happen?

God will still be on the throne, and we'll need the real-life rest He offers more than ever. That's why I chose Psalm 80:18 as the scripture for this Conclusion: "Then we will not turn away from you; revive us, and we will call on your name."

The reality is that even in the best of times, we never know when life will be drastically, irreversibly, or permanently interrupted. But this is nothing new. In John 16:33, after sharing with His disciples some personally frightening future events, Jesus then comforts them with these words: "I have told you these things, so that *in me* you may have peace. In this world you will have trouble. But take heart! I have overcome the world" (emphasis added).

Even as this book started with the story of God's creation, we must acknowledge that from time's first moment, all He created has been moving toward a final conclusion. Doesn't it make sense, then, that seeking Sabbath rest is more important than ever? Like never before, we need space in our lives reserved for worshiping the Creator, for processing and applying all we've learned, for examining and enjoying what we've created, for sorting and deciding what's worth keeping and what we need to discard.

That's why, starting with our sabbatical, Jim and I have spent increasingly more time evaluating what we're doing, why we're doing it, and how much longer we intend to keep it up. Admittedly, this is partly because we're getting older, and the older you get the more unencumbered you want to be. As my friend Cecile Murphy wrote in a recent newsletter, "Maybe that's why God created our bodies to wear out—so we're forced to slow down, to do less, and to appreciate the quiet moments of life."

Frankly, though, it's kind of nice when we reach the place at which we can stop worrying so much about warranties and start letting go of a lot of earthly entanglements.

This includes the curse of too much stuff. Like many others, come the new year I'm planning to do some major de-cluttering. For incentive, I've chosen a verse from 1 Corinthians 14:33— "God is not a God of disorder but of peace." If I read this right, it indicates that cutting the clutter—both material and spiritual—is yet another good path toward pursuing peace.

The reality is that, young or old, we don't know how many moments we have left. That's why we must focus more on living in *this* moment. The only way to do that is by trading intensity for intentionality. According to a quote attributed to late *Family Circus* cartoonist Bil Keane, it could be the greatest gift we ever give ourselves: "The past is history, the future is a mystery, today is a gift. That's why they call it the present"—one we get to open every single day.

So as the year comes to a conclusion, finally this book does too. In the end it has taken me two full years to finish, longer than any I've previously written. My prayer is that the "sabbatitudes" shared will lead us all to religiously pursue Sabbath rest and by doing so come to a more peaceful conclusion not only now on earth but eventually in heaven as well.

We can start by taking a lot more sunrise snapshots.

NOTES

Chapter 2

1. Watchman Nee, *A Table in the Wilderness* (Fort Washington, Pa.: CLC Publications, 2000), July 8 devotional.

2. Cynthia Ramnarace, "7 Daily Tricks to Fight a Frazzled Brain," <www.everydayhealth.com>. Accessed June 20, 2011.

Chapter 4

1. S. I. McMillen and David E. Stern, *None of These Diseases,* updated edition (Ada, Mich.: Revell, 2000).

2. Abigail L. Cuffey, "Meditation on the Go," *Woman's Day,* November 7, 2010, 92.

3. Ramnarace, "7 Daily Tricks to Fight a Frazzled Brain."

Chapter 5

1. Mary Duenwald, "The Importance of Doing Nothing," *Martha Stewart Living,* June 2011, 155, 157.

Chapter 6

1. Carl Honore, *In Praise of Slowness* (New York: Harper Collins, 2005).

2. Joyce Meyers, *Eat the Cookie . . . Buy the Shoes* (New York: FaithWords, New York, 2010) 36-38.

3. Wendy Connell, "Christian Book Summaries," <www.christianbooksummaries.com>, vol. 3, no. 19.

4. George Howe Colt, *The Big House: A Century in the Life of an American Summer Home* (New York: Scribner, 2003), 236.

5. Judi Braddy, *Camp Gramma: Putting Down Spiritual Stakes for Your Grandchildren* (Kansas City: Beacon Hill Press of Kansas City, 2009).

Chapter 7

1. Sue Ellin Browder, "You Gotta Have Friends," *Woman's Day,* April 2006, 46.

2. Judi Braddy, *It All Comes Out in the Wash: Sorting Through Priorities When Your Life Is Out of Balance* (Kansas City: Beacon Hill Press of Kansas City, 2006), 160-61.

3. Denise Foley, "The Secret of Beating Fatigue," *Good Housekeeping*, January 2012, 45.

Chapter 8

1. Nancie Carmichael, "Selah," *Woman's Touch* magazine, July-August 2004, 14-15.

2. Robin Lee Hatcher, "Write Thinking," Blogspot, <www.robinlee hatcher.com>. Accessed March 11, 2011.

Chapter 9

1. Ken Brandon, "Believing the Promises," <www.brandonweb.com/sermons/sermonpages/2corinthians6.htm>. Accessed March 20, 2013.

Chapter 10

1. Gay Norton Edelman, "Be Happy Now," *Family Circle*, Winter 2012.

2. "Father Richard's Daily Meditations" (Center for Action and Contemplation, <cacradicalgrace.org>. Accessed January 24, 2012.

3. Lisa Jones, "Got Gratitude?" *Woman's Day*, November 2010.

4. Excerpted from *The American Heritage Dictionary of the English Language*, Third Edition, 1992 by Houghton Mifflin Company.

5. Brother Lawrence, "The Practice of the Presence of God" (Create Space Independent Publishing Platform, (Ada, Mich.: Revell, 1967).

6. Lynne Chandler, "Wow What a Ride!" Women in Ministry Mobilized, <www.womeninministry.ag.org,> June 18, 2010.

Chapter 11

1. Excerpted from *The American Heritage Dictionary of the English Language*, Third Edition, 1992 by Houghton Mifflin Company.

BIBLIOGRAPHY

Baab, Lynn. *Sabbath Keeping: Finding Freedom in the Rythms of Rest* (Westmont, Ill.: InterVarsity Press, 2005).

Breathnach, Sarah Ban. *Simple Abundance: A Daybook of Comfort and Joy,* reissue edition (New York: Grand Central Publishing, 2009).

Buchanan, Mark. *The Rest of God: Restoring Your Soul by Restoring Sabbath* (Nashville: Thomas Nelson, 2007).

Carmichael, Nancie. *Selah: Your Moment to Stop, Think and Step into Your Future* (Ada, Mich.: Revell, 2004).

Cloud, Henry and Townsend, John, *Safe People: How to Find Relationships that Are Good for You and Avoid Those that Aren't,* (Zondervan, Grand Rapids, Mich., 1995).

Colt, George Howe. *The Big House: A Century in the Life of an American Summer Home* (New York: Scribner, 2003).

Foster, Richard. *Freedom of Simplicity: Finding Harmony in a Complex World,* reprint (New York: HarperOne, 2005).

Gire, Ken. *Windows of the Soul: Experiencing God in New Ways* (Grand Rapids, Mich.: Zondervan Publishing House, 1996).

Honore, Carl. *In Praise of Slowness* (New York: Harper Collins, 2005).

Kent, Keri Wyatt. *Rest: Living in Sabbath Simplicity* (New York: Zondervan Publishing House, 2008).

McMillen, S. I., and David E. Stern. *None of These Diseases,* updated edition (Ada, Mich.: Revell, 2000). Note: The original text by S.I. McMillen (Spire Books, 1963) is still available.

Meyers, Joyce. *Eat the Cookie . . . Buy the Shoes* (New York: FaithWords, Hachette Book Group, 2010).

Muller, Wayne. *Sabbath: Finding Rest, Renewal and Delight in Our Busy Lives* (New York: Bantam, 2000).

———. *Sabbath: Restoring the Sacred Rhythm of Rest* (New York: Bantam, 1999).

Nee, Watchman. *A Table in the Wilderness* (Fort Washington, Pa.: CLC Publications, 2000).

Wheeler, Claire M. *10 Simple Solutions to Stress: How to Tame Tension and Start Enjoying Your Life* (Oakland, Calif.: New Harbinger Publications, 2007).

Winner, Lauren F. *Mudhouse Sabbath: An Invitation to a Life of Spiritual Discipline* (Brewster, Mass.: Paraclete Press, 2007).

Wirzba, Norman. *Living the Sabbath: Discovering the Rhythms of Rest and Delight* (Ada, Mich.: Brazos Press, 2006).

Classics

à Kempis, Thomas. *The Imitation of Christ* (New York: Simon & Brown, 2013).

Hurnard, Hannah. *Hinds' Feet on High Places* (Radford, Va.: Wilder Publications, 2012).

Lawrence, Brother, *The Practice of the Presence of God,* (Revell, reprinted edition, February, 1967).

Munger, Robert Boyd, *My Heart, Christ's Home* (InterVarsity Press, Downer's Grove, Ill., 1992).

Nouwen, Henri J. M. *The Way of the Heart* (New York: Ballantine Books, 2003).

Tozer, A. W. *The Pursuit of God* (Greensboro, N.C.: WLC, 2009).

Navigate
the unexpected

With humor and refreshing honesty, author Judi
Braddy shares the true north points she learned
while living in Alaska and explains how these
points have helped her keep her bearings—
even through life's most battering storms.

True North
Staying on Course Through Life's Changing Circumstances
Judi Braddy

ISBN: 978-0-8341-2341-0

Available wherever books are sold

BEACON HILL PRESS
OF KANSAS CITY

Life is a lot like laundry.
It piles up quickly and can get really stinky.

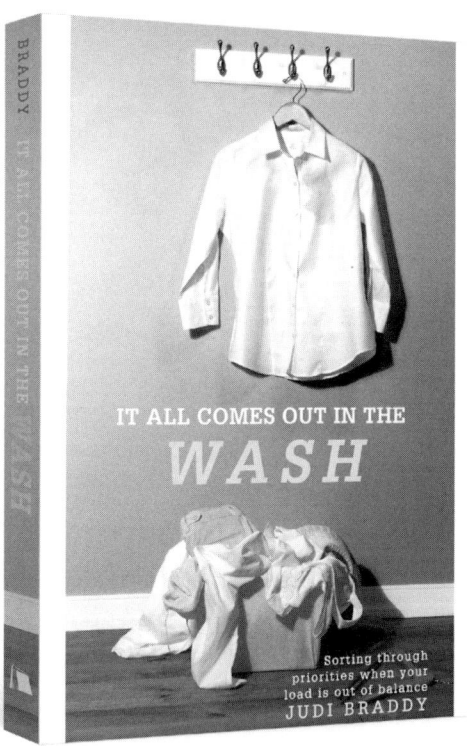

If you don't follow the maker's instructions, or if you overload
your life, what should be dazzling-clean ends up stained and dingy.
With insight, wit, and humor, Judi Braddy challenges
you to discover the difference between *doing* it all
and *becoming* all God created you to be.

It All Comes Out in the Wash
ISBN: 978-0-8341-2259-8

BEACON HILL PRESS
OF KANSAS CITY
Available online at BeaconHillBooks.com